New Asian
The food of Thailand·Vietnam·China·Japan

THE AUSTRALIAN
Women's Weekly

contents

Our love of travel and the influences of migration have caused real changes in our traditional eating habits, with the biggest and most recent impact coming from Asia. Chinese, Thai, Vietnamese, Japanese and Malaysian cooking are second nature to us now, and the wealth of new ingredients introduced from these countries has created a total rethink about the way we eat today. Here's a yummy sampler of the best new Asian food we can call our own.

Pamela Clark
Food Director

the flavours of asia

For many of us growing up, Asian food extended only as far as the local Chinese takeaway shop's menu – honey chicken, "special" fried rice and perhaps even a beef in black bean sauce. Thankfully, those days are well and truly in the past and we are now part of an era where Asian food, not just Chinese but Thai, Vietnamese, Indian and Japanese, too, all play a great role in the way we eat. Cooking dinner for the family, eating solo or catering for crowds is possible to do with these recipes. We've spent a great deal of time developing and testing the new flavours of Asia; however, our job has been made easier thanks to the fantastic range of Asian herbs, spices, noodles and the like available today. We've discovered that you no longer have to venture far to fill a basket with ingredients such as fresh lemon grass, galangal and thai basil. Armed with our easy-to-follow recipes, a bunch of quality supplies and a stove that's ready to go, you'll find new Asian food not only a cinch to make, but enjoyable and, best of all, some of the yummiest food to ever hit your lips.

Asian ingredients

VIETNAMESE MINT is not a mint at all, but a pungent and peppery narrow-leafed member of the buckwheat family. Not confined to Vietnam, it is also known as cambodian mint, pak pai (Thailand), laksa leaf (Indonesia), daun kesom (Singapore), and rau ram in Vietnam. It is a common ingredient in Asian foods, particularly soups, salads and stir-fries.

WOMBOK, also known as chinese cabbage, peking cabbage, wong bok or petsai. Elongated in shape with pale green, crinkly leaves, this is the most common cabbage in South-East Asia, forming the basis of the pickled Korean condiment, kim chi, and providing the crunch in Vietnamese rice paper rolls. Can be shredded or chopped and eaten raw or braised, steamed or stir-fried.

KAFFIR LIME LEAVES, also known as bai magrood; look like two glossy dark-green leaves joined end to end, forming a rounded hourglass shape. Used fresh or dried, like bay leaves or curry leaves, in many Asian dishes. Sold fresh, dried or frozen, the dried leaves are less potent so double the number called for in a recipe if you substitute them for fresh leaves. A strip of fresh lime peel may be substituted for each kaffir lime leaf.

TURMERIC, also known as kamin; is a rhizome related to galangal and ginger, must be grated or pounded to release its somewhat acrid aroma and pungent flavour. Known for the golden colour it imparts to dishes. Fresh turmeric can be substituted with the more common dried powder (use 2 teaspoons of ground turmeric plus a teaspoon of sugar for every 20g of fresh turmeric called for in a recipe).

GAI LAN is a member of the cabbage family, and is also known as chinese kale, chinese broccoli and gai larn; this green vegetable is appreciated more for its stems than its coarse leaves. It is similar in texture to regular broccoli, but milder in taste. Gai lan can be served steamed and stir-fried, in soups and noodle dishes.

BUK CHOY, also known as bok choy, pak choi, chinese white cabbage or chinese chard; has a fresh, mild mustard taste. Use both stems and leaves, stir-fried or braised. Baby buk choy, also known as pak kat farang or shanghai bok choy, is much smaller and more tender than buk choy.

LEMON GRASS, also known as takrai, serai or serah. A tall, clumping, lemon-smelling and tasting, sharp-edged aromatic tropical grass; the white lower part of the stem is used, finely chopped, in much of the cooking of South-East Asia. Can be found, fresh, dried, powdered and frozen, in supermarkets and greengrocers, as well as Asian food stores.

NORI is a type of dried seaweed used in Japanese cooking as a flavouring, garnish or to make sushi. Sold in thin sheets, plain or toasted (yaki-nori). The thin, dark sheets are usually a dark purplish-black, but they turn green and acquire a pleasant, nutty flavour when toasted. It is available from Asian food stores and most supermarkets.

DAIKON is an everyday fixture at the Japanese table; this long, white horseradish has a wonderful, sweet flavour. After peeling, eat it raw in salads or shredded as a garnish; it is also great when sliced or cubed and cooked in stir-fries and casseroles. The flesh is white, but the skin can be either white or black; buy those that are firm and unwrinkled from Asian food stores.

GALANGAL, also known as ka or lengkaus if fresh and laos if dried and powdered. A rhizome with a hot ginger-citrusy flavour; it looks like ginger but is dense and fibrous and harder to cut. Used similarly to ginger and garlic as a seasoning and as an ingredient. Fresh ginger can be substituted for fresh galangal, but the flavour of the dish will not be the same.

WATER CHESTNUTS resemble chestnuts in appearance, hence the English name. They are small brown tubers with a crisp, white, nutty-tasting flesh. Their crunchy texture is best experienced fresh, however, canned water chestnuts are more easily obtained and can be kept about a month, once opened, under refrigeration.

THAI BASIL is also known as horapa; it's different from holy basil and sweet basil in both look and taste, having smaller leaves and purplish stems. It has a slight aniseed taste and is one of the identifying flavours of Thai food. This basil is available from Asian food stores, some specialist fruit and vegetable shops and supermarkets.

soups + starters

pho bo

preparation time 20 minutes | cooking time 1 hour 20 minutes | serves 6

Large bowls of pho (noodle soup) are a breakfast favourite throughout Vietnam, but we like to eat it any time of the day. Round steak, gravy beef (shin) and skirt steak are all suitable for this recipe.

2 litres (8 cups) water
1 litre (4 cups) beef stock
1kg beef chuck steak
2 star anise
8cm piece fresh ginger (40g), grated
⅓ cup (80ml) japanese soy sauce
200g bean thread noodles
1½ cups (120g) bean sprouts
¼ cup loosely packed fresh coriander leaves
⅓ cup loosely packed fresh mint leaves
4 green onions, sliced thinly
2 fresh long red chillies, sliced thinly
¼ cup (60ml) fish sauce
1 lime, cut into wedges

1 Place the water and stock in large saucepan with beef, star anise, ginger and soy sauce; bring to a boil. Reduce heat; simmer, covered, 30 minutes. Uncover; simmer about 30 minutes or until beef is tender.

2 Meanwhile, place noodles in medium heatproof bowl, cover with boiling water; stand until just tender, drain.

3 Combine sprouts, herbs, onion and chilli in medium bowl.

4 Remove beef from pan. Strain broth through muslin-lined sieve or colander into large heatproof bowl; discard solids. When beef is cool enough to handle, remove and discard fat and sinew. Slice beef thinly, return to same cleaned pan with broth; bring to a boil. Stir in fish sauce.

5 Divide noodles among soup bowls; ladle hot beef broth into bowls, sprinkle with sprout mixture and serve with lime wedges.
per serving 13.8g total fat (6.2g saturated fat); 1601kJ (383 cal); 21g carbohydrate; 41.3g protein; 4.1g fibre

duck and green onion gyoza

preparation time 40 minutes | cooking time 20 minutes | makes 30

1kg chinese barbecued duck
4 green onions, sliced thinly
1 tablespoon japanese soy sauce
2 tablespoons cooking sake
2cm piece fresh ginger (10g), grated
1 fresh long red chilli, chopped finely
30 gyoza wrappers
2 tablespoons vegetable oil

sake dipping sauce
¼ cup (60ml) cooking sake
2 tablespoons japanese soy sauce
1 tablespoon lime juice
1 teaspoon caster sugar

1   Remove and discard skin and bones from duck; chop meat finely. Combine duck, onion, sauce, sake, ginger and chilli in medium bowl.

2   Place one heaped teaspoon of duck mixture in centre of one wrapper; wet edge around one half of wrapper. Pleat to seal. Repeat with remaining duck mixture and wrappers.

3   Cover base of large frying pan with water; bring to a boil then add gyoza, in batches. Reduce heat, simmer, covered, 3 minutes.

4   Meanwhile, make sake dipping sauce.

5   Heat oil in same cleaned pan; cook gyoza on one side only, uncovered, in batches, until browned and slightly crisp. Drain on absorbent paper. Serve immediately with sake dipping sauce.

sake dipping sauce   Combine ingredients in screw-top jar; shake well.

per gyoza 6.3g total fat (1.7g saturated); 393kJ (94 cal); 4.9g carbohydrate; 3.9g protein; 0g fibre

GYOZA WRAPPERS *are thin pastry rounds made from wheat flour that the Japanese use to wrap around fillings for dumplings and pot stickers. If unavailable, substitute gow gee wrappers.*

thai crab and mango salad

preparation time 20 minutes | serves 4

*You can use an equal weight of prawns or lobster instead
of the crab meat in this salad.*
*Make sure your mango is quite firm, otherwise it will not
slice well.*

500g fresh crab meat
1 firm medium mango (430g)
100g mizuna
1 cup loosely packed fresh mint leaves
lime and chilli dressing
⅓ cup (80ml) lime juice
2 fresh long red chillies, sliced thinly
5cm piece fresh ginger (25g), cut into matchsticks
2 shallots (50g), sliced thinly
1 tablespoon fish sauce
2 tablespoons grated palm sugar
2 teaspoons peanut oil

1   Make lime and chilli dressing.
2   Combine crab in medium bowl with half the dressing.
3   Using vegetable peeler, slice mango into thin strips. Combine
mango, mizuna and mint in large bowl with remaining dressing.
4   Divide salad among serving plates; top with crab.
lime and chilli dressing   Combine ingredients in screw-top jar;
shake well.
per serving   3.5g total fat (0.6g saturated fat); 790kJ (189 cal);
19.4g carbohydrate; 18g protein; 3g fibre

ramen, pork and spinach soup

preparation time 20 minutes (plus refrigeration time) | cooking time 1 hour 15 minutes | serves 4

*It's best to make the broth the day before you want to eat the
soup, so that it can chill long enough for the fat to solidify on
top. Scoop it away and discard it for a beautifully clear broth.*

1kg chicken necks
3 litres (12 cups) water
1 large leek (500g), chopped coarsely
5cm piece fresh ginger (25g), sliced thinly
10 black peppercorns
250g fresh ramen noodles
¼ cup (60ml) japanese soy sauce
¼ cup (60ml) cooking sake
1 teaspoon sesame oil
300g spinach, trimmed, chopped coarsely
200g piece chinese barbecued pork, sliced thinly
1 fresh long red chilli, sliced thinly
½ sheet nori, cut into 2cm pieces

1   Combine chicken, the water, leek, ginger and peppercorns
in large saucepan; bring to a boil. Reduce heat; simmer,
uncovered, 1 hour. Strain broth through muslin-lined sieve into
large heatproof bowl; discard solids. Allow broth to cool; cover.
Refrigerate until cold.
2   Place noodles in large heatproof bowl, cover with boiling
water; separate with fork, stand 2 minutes, drain.
3   Skim and discard fat from surface of broth; return to same
cleaned pan, bring to a boil. Stir in sauce, sake and oil; return
to a boil. Remove from heat.
4   Divide noodles, spinach, pork, chilli and nori among serving
bowls; ladle broth into bowls.
per serving   12.4g total fat (4.8g saturated fat); 1680kJ (402 cal);
40.1g carbohydrate; 26.6g protein; 4.5g fibre

chicken and water chestnut tofu pouches

preparation time 25 minutes | cooking time 20 minutes | serves 4

Tonkatsu, a thick, fruity, spicy sauce, somewhat similar to a commercial barbecue sauce, is available from Asian grocery stores.

500g chicken mince
⅓ cup (65g) water chestnuts, rinsed,
    drained, chopped finely
¼ teaspoon five-spice
1 tablespoon finely chopped fresh coriander
1 clove garlic, crushed
2cm piece fresh ginger (10g), grated
1 fresh long red chilli, chopped finely
12 seasoned fried bean curd pouches
⅓ cup (80ml) tonkatsu sauce

1   Combine mince, chestnut, five-spice, coriander, garlic, ginger and chilli in medium bowl.

2   Carefully open pouches on one side, gently pushing fingers into each corner.

3   Spoon one rounded tablespoon of chicken mixture into pouch, pushing mixture into corners (be careful not to overfill or tear pouch). Fold one side of pouch down over chicken mixture; fold other side over top of first side. Turn pouch over so fold is underneath. Repeat with remaining pouches and mixture.

4   Place pouches, in single layer, in baking-paper-lined bamboo steamer. Steam, covered, over wok of simmering water, about 15 minutes or until cooked through.

5   Cook pouches in heated lightly oiled large frying pan, uncovered, about 5 minutes or until browned. Serve pouches with tonkatsu sauce.

per serving 15.4g total fat (4.2g saturated fat); 1233kJ (295 cal); 8.4g carbohydrate; 29.2g protein; 3.6g fibre

BEAN CURD POUCHES *Ready-to-use seasoned bean curd pouches are available cryovac-packed from Asian supermarkets.*

chilli squid salad

preparation time 15 minutes | cooking time 10 minutes | serves 4

3 cleaned squid hoods (450g)
1 tablespoon sweet chilli sauce
2 teaspoons fish sauce
2 teaspoons lime juice
1 tablespoon peanut oil
1 telegraph cucumber (400g),
    halved lengthways, sliced thinly
3 green onions, sliced thinly
1 cup (80g) bean sprouts
¼ cup firmly packed fresh coriander leaves
⅓ cup firmly packed fresh mint leaves
1 fresh long red chilli, sliced thinly
¼ cup (60ml) sweet chilli sauce, extra
1 tablespoon lime juice, extra

1   Cut squid hoods in half lengthways; score inside in diagonal pattern. Cut each half in four pieces.

2   Combine squid, sauces and juice in medium bowl.

3   Heat oil in wok; stir-fry squid, in batches, until cooked through. Combine squid in large bowl with remaining ingredients.

per serving 6.6g total fat (1.4g saturated fat); 744kJ (178 cal); 6.5g carbohydrate; 21.4g protein; 3g fibre

pork and garlic chive wrapped prawns

preparation time 30 minutes | cooking time 15 minutes | serves 4

250g pork mince
2 tablespoons finely chopped fresh garlic chives
1 fresh small red thai chilli, chopped finely
2cm piece fresh ginger (10g), grated
12 uncooked large king prawns (840g)
12 x 12cm-square spring roll wrappers
2 tablespoons cornflour
¼ cup (60ml) water
peanut oil, for deep-frying

1   Combine mince, chives, chilli and ginger in medium bowl.

2   Shell and devein prawns, leaving tails intact. Cut along back of each prawn, without cutting all the way through; flatten prawns slightly.

3   Place spring roll wrapper on board; fold one corner up to meet centre. Place one flattened prawn onto wrapper; top prawn with 1 level tablespoon pork mixture. Brush around edges with blended cornflour and the water. Fold wrapper around filling, leaving tail exposed; press edges together to seal. Repeat with remaining prawns, pork mixture and wrappers.

4   Heat oil in wok; deep-fry prawns, in batches, until cooked. Drain on absorbent paper.

per serving 15.7g total fat (3.7g saturated); 1359kJ (325 cal); 10.6g carbohydrate; 35.1g protein; 0.4g fibre

goes well with sweet chilli or soy sauce.

salt and pepper quail with herb salad

preparation time 30 minutes | cooking time 20 minutes | serves 4

6 quails (960g)
½ cup (75g) plain flour
1½ tablespoons sea salt flakes
2 teaspoons coarsely ground black pepper
vegetable oil, for deep-frying
lemon pepper dipping sauce
¼ cup (60ml) vegetable oil
1 teaspoon finely grated lemon rind
⅓ cup (80ml) lemon juice
2 tablespoons grated palm sugar
1 teaspoon ground white pepper
herb salad
½ cup loosely packed vietnamese mint leaves
½ cup loosely packed fresh coriander leaves
1 cup (80g) bean sprouts
1 fresh long red chilli, sliced thinly

1 Rinse quails under cold water; pat dry. Discard necks from quails. Using kitchen scissors, cut along sides of each quail's backbone; discard backbones. Halve each quail along breastbone.

2 Make lemon pepper dipping sauce. Make herb salad.

3 Combine flour, salt and pepper in large bowl. Add quail; coat quail in flour mixture. Shake off excess.

4 Heat oil in wok; deep-fry quail, in batches, about 6 minutes or until quail is cooked. Drain on absorbent paper.

5 Divide quail among serving plates; top with herb salad. Serve with remaining dipping sauce.

lemon pepper dipping sauce Combine ingredients in screw-top jar; shake well.

herb salad Combine ingredients in medium bowl with 1 tablespoon of the lemon pepper dipping sauce.

per serving 34.8g total fat (6.2g saturated); 2098kJ (502 cal); 21.4g carbohydrate; 25.5g protein; 2g fibre

tip | Quail, the smallest of the game birds, is available from butchers and some supermarkets. It makes for a perfect starter due to its delicate, yet flavoursome nature. This recipe is best prepared just before serving.

chicken and yellow bean relish

preparation time 10 minutes | cooking time 10 minutes | makes 1 cup

Due to the richness of this relish, you only need to serve a small amount to enjoy its delicious flavour.

3 cloves garlic, quartered
2 purple shallots (50g), chopped coarsely
1 tablespoon vegetable oil
2 tablespoons yellow bean paste
150g chicken mince
⅓ cup (80ml) coconut cream
2 tablespoons chicken stock
¼ teaspoon dried chilli flakes
⅓ cup loosely packed fresh coriander leaves
⅓ cup coarsely chopped fresh mint
8 large trimmed wombok leaves

1 Using mortar and pestle, crush garlic and shallot until mixture forms a paste.

2 Heat oil in wok; stir-fry garlic mixture until browned lightly. Add paste; stir-fry until fragrant.

3 Add mince to wok; stir-fry until cooked through. Add coconut cream, stock and chilli; bring to a boil. Reduce heat; simmer, uncovered, about 5 minutes or until thickened. Remove from heat; stir in herbs.

4 Serve relish with wombok leaves, sliced cucumber and carrot sticks, if you like.

per tablespoon 4.1g total fat (1.7g saturated); 238kJ (57 cal); 1.4g carbohydrate; 3.4g protein; 1g fibre

PURPLE SHALLOTS *are also known as Asian shallots; related to the onion, but resembling garlic, they grow in bulbs of multiple cloves. Thin-layered and intensely flavoured, they are used in cooking throughout South-East Asia.*

seafood

grilled salmon with nam jim and herb salad

preparation time 30 minutes | cooking time 10 minutes | serves 4

Nam jim is a generic term for a Thai dipping sauce; most versions include fish sauce and chillies, but the remaining ingredients are up to the cook's discretion.

4 x 220g salmon fillets, skin-on

nam jim

3 long green chillies, chopped coarsely

2 fresh small red thai chillies, chopped coarsely

2 cloves garlic, quartered

1 shallot (25g), quartered

2cm piece fresh ginger (10g), quartered

⅓ cup (80ml) lime juice

2 tablespoons fish sauce

1 tablespoon grated palm sugar

1 tablespoon peanut oil

¼ cup (35g) roasted unsalted cashews, chopped finely

herb salad

1½ cups loosely packed fresh mint leaves

1 cup loosely packed fresh coriander leaves

1 cup loosely packed fresh basil leaves, torn

1 medium red onion (170g), sliced thinly

2 lebanese cucumbers (260g), seeded, sliced thinly

1   Make nam jim.

2   Cook salmon, both sides, on heated oiled grill plate (or grill or barbecue) until cooked as desired.

3   Meanwhile, combine ingredients for herb salad in medium bowl.

4   Serve salmon and herb salad topped with nam jim.

nam jim Blend or process chillies, garlic, shallot, ginger, juice, sauce, sugar and oil until smooth; stir in nuts.

per serving 25g total fat (5.1g saturated fat); 1948kJ (466 cal); 10.8g carbohydrate; 47.6g protein; 4.4g fibre

lemon grass fish with daikon salad

preparation time 10 minutes | cooking time 20 minutes | serves 4

While we used small snapper here, you can also use small bream or any other plate-sized whole fish in this recipe.

4 small whole snapper (1.5kg)
1 medium brown onion (150g), chopped coarsely
1 clove garlic, quartered
2cm piece fresh ginger (10g), quartered
10cm stick fresh lemon grass (20g), sliced thinly
2 tablespoons tamarind concentrate
1 tablespoon brown sugar
1 tablespoon sambal oelek
1 tablespoon kecap manis
2 teaspoons peanut oil
½ cup (125ml) water
1 small daikon (400g), cut into matchsticks
1 medium carrot (120g), cut into matchsticks
½ cup loosely packed fresh coriander leaves

1 Preheat oven to 200°C/180°C fan-forced.

2 Using sharp knife, score each fish three times on each side through thickest part of flesh; place fish in large oiled shallow baking dish.

3 Blend or process onion, garlic, ginger, lemon grass, tamarind, sugar, sambal and kecap manis until mixture forms a smooth paste.

4 Heat oil in small frying pan; cook paste, stirring, 5 minutes. Add the water; bring to a boil. Reduce heat; simmer, uncovered, 2 minutes.

5 Brush half the sauce inside each fish; pour remaining sauce over fish. Roast, uncovered, brushing occasionally, about 15 minutes or until fish is cooked.

6 Meanwhile, combine daikon, carrot and half the coriander in medium bowl.

7 Serve fish sprinkled with remaining coriander, and daikon salad.

per serving 5g total fat (1.3g saturated); 949kJ (227 cal); 12.6g carbohydrate; 30.9g protein; 3.2g fibre

spiced coconut prawn stir-fry

preparation time 10 minutes | cooking time 10 minutes | serves 4

1.25kg uncooked medium king prawns
500g cauliflower, cut into florets
200g broccoli, cut into florets
1 medium brown onion (150g), sliced thinly
2 cloves garlic, sliced thinly
2 fresh long red chillies, sliced thinly
1 teaspoon ground turmeric
2 teaspoons yellow mustard seeds
¼ teaspoon ground cardamom
½ teaspoon ground cumin
140ml can coconut milk
2 tablespoons mango chutney

1 Shell and devein prawns, leaving tails intact. Combine prawns and remaining ingredients in large bowl.

2 Stir-fry ingredients in heated oiled wok until vegetables are just tender.

per serving 8.7g total fat (6.5g saturated fat); 1225kJ (293 cal); 11.9g carbohydrate; 38.5g protein; 6g fibre

goes well with steamed jasmine rice.

prawn laksa

preparation time 30 minutes | cooking time 45 minutes | serves 4

1 tablespoon vegetable oil

2 x 400ml cans coconut milk

1 litre (4 cups) chicken stock

1 tablespoon brown sugar

2 teaspoons fish sauce

6 fresh kaffir lime leaves, shredded finely

1kg uncooked medium king prawns

250g fresh thin egg noodles

125g dried thin rice noodles

1 cup (80g) bean sprouts

¼ cup loosely packed fresh coriander leaves

1 lime, quartered

laksa paste

1 medium brown onion (150g), chopped coarsely

⅓ cup (80ml) coconut milk

2 tablespoons lime juice

1 tablespoon shrimp paste

2cm piece fresh ginger (10g), grated

1 tablespoon macadamias (10g), halved

10cm stick fresh lemon grass (20g), chopped finely

4 cloves garlic, quartered

2 fresh small red thai chillies, chopped coarsely

2 teaspoons ground coriander

2 teaspoons ground cumin

1 teaspoon ground turmeric

1 Make laksa paste.

2 Heat oil in large saucepan; cook laksa paste, stirring, about 5 minutes or until fragrant. Add coconut milk, stock, sugar, sauce and lime leaves; bring to a boil. Reduce heat; simmer, covered, 30 minutes.

3 Meanwhile, shell and devein prawns, leaving tails intact.

4 Place egg noodles in medium heatproof bowl, cover with boiling water; separate with fork, drain. Place rice noodles in same bowl, cover with boiling water; stand until just tender, drain.

5 Add prawns to laksa; cook, uncovered, until just changed in colour.

6 Divide noodles among serving bowls; ladle hot laksa into bowls. Top with sprouts and coriander; serve with lime.

laksa paste Blend or process ingredients until mixture forms a smooth paste.

per serving 55.2g total fat (41.6g saturated fat); 3775kJ (903 cal); 56.6g carbohydrate; 42g protein; 7.6g fibre

SHRIMP PASTE *also known as trasi or blanchan; it is a strong-scented, very firm preserved paste made of salted dried shrimp. Used as a pungent flavouring in many South-East Asian soups and sauces.*

garlic and chilli seafood stir-fry

preparation time 25 minutes | cooking time 20 minutes | serves 4

720g uncooked medium king prawns

2 cleaned squid hoods (300g)

540g octopus, quartered

¼ cup (60ml) peanut oil

6 cloves garlic, sliced thinly

2cm piece fresh ginger (10g), sliced thinly

2 fresh long red chillies, sliced thinly

2 tablespoons chinese cooking wine

1 teaspoon caster sugar

4 green onions, cut in 4cm pieces

chilli fried shallots

1 tablespoon fried shallots

1 teaspoon sea salt flakes

½ teaspoon dried chilli flakes

1 Shell and devein prawns, leaving tails intact. Cut squid down centre to open out; score inside in diagonal pattern then cut into thick strips. Quarter octopus lengthways.

2 Combine ingredients for chilli fried shallots in small bowl.

3 Heat 1 tablespoon of the oil in wok; stir-fry prawns until changed in colour, remove from wok. Heat another tablespoon of the oil in wok; stir-fry squid until cooked through, remove from wok. Heat remaining oil in wok; stir-fry octopus until tender.

4 Stir-fry garlic, ginger and chilli in wok until fragrant. Return seafood to wok with remaining ingredients; stir-fry until hot.

5 Serve stir-fry sprinkled with chilli shallots.

per serving 4.7g total fat (0.8g saturated fat); 460kJ (110 cal); 0.8g carbohydrate; 15.5g protein; 0.3g fibre

banana-leaf steamed fish

preparation time 30 minutes | cooking time 20 minutes | serves 4

While we used small bream here, you can also use small snapper or any other plate-sized whole fish in this recipe.

3 large banana leaves

3cm piece fresh galangal (15g), quartered

2 shallots (50g), quartered

2 cloves garlic

1 tablespoon fish sauce

¼ cup (60ml) lime juice

2 tablespoons peanut oil

2 x 10cm sticks fresh lemon grass (40g)

4 x 240g whole bream

⅓ cup firmly packed fresh coriander leaves

¼ cup coarsely chopped vietnamese mint

1 fresh long red chilli, sliced thinly

4 green onions, sliced thinly

1 lime, quartered

1 Trim two banana leaves into four 30cm x 40cm rectangles. Using metal tongs, dip one piece at a time into large saucepan of boiling water; remove immediately. Rinse under cold water; pat dry with absorbent paper. Trim remaining banana leaf to fit grill plate (or grill or barbecue).

2 Blend or process galangal, shallot, garlic, sauce, juice and oil. Strain dressing into small bowl; discard solids.

3 Place banana leaves on bench. Halve lemon grass lengthways then crossways.

4 Score fish both sides through thickest part of flesh. Place two pieces of cut lemon grass on each leaf; place one fish on top of lemon grass, top with equal amounts of dressing. Fold opposite corners of each leaf into centre to enclose fish; secure parcel at 5cm intervals with kitchen string.

5 Place remaining leaf pieces onto heated grill plate (or grill or barbecue); place parcels on leaf. Cook, turning halfway through cooking time, about 20 minutes or until fish is cooked as desired.

6 Meanwhile, combine herbs, chilli and onion in small bowl.

7 Open parcels; serve fish sprinkled with herb mixture and lime.

per serving 16.4g total fat (4.1g saturated fat); 1150kJ (275 cal); 3.2g carbohydrate; 28.2g protein; 1.7g fibre

tip

Luscious, ripe mango works well with this recipe, too. Substitute half a thinly sliced small mango for the fresh coconut in the salad, if you like. Leftover coconut can be used for beef carpaccio with green papaya salad (see page 73).

thai coconut scallops

preparation time 25 minutes | cooking time 25 minutes | serves 4

You will need a small fresh coconut for this recipe. To open it, preheat oven to 240°C/ 220°C fan-forced. Pierce one of the eyes of the coconut with a sharp knife; place on oven tray. Roast 10 minutes or until cracks appear; remove from oven. When cool enough to handle, pull coconut apart. Use only the firm white flesh you find inside.

2 tablespoons peanut oil

24 scallops without roe (600g)

1 shallot (25g), chopped finely

2cm piece fresh ginger (10g), grated

2 cloves garlic, crushed

2 tablespoons red curry paste

400ml can coconut milk

1 tablespoon fish sauce

1 tablespoon lime juice

1 tablespoon grated palm sugar

1 fresh kaffir lime leaf, torn

herb salad

½ cup loosely packed fresh mint leaves

½ cup loosely packed thai basil leaves

½ cup (40g) shaved fresh coconut

2 fresh long red chillies, shredded finely

1 green onion, sliced thinly

1 Combine ingredients for herb salad in large bowl.

2 Heat half the oil in medium frying pan; cook scallops, in batches, until browned.

3 Heat remaining oil in same pan; cook shallot, ginger and garlic, stirring, until shallot softens. Add paste; cook, stirring, until fragrant. Add coconut milk, sauce, juice, sugar and lime leaf; bring to a boil. Reduce heat; simmer, uncovered, about 5 minutes or until sauce thickens slightly. Add scallops; reheat gently.

4 Divide scallops among serving plates, pour sauce around scallops; serve with salad.

per serving 37.8g total fat (22.9g saturated fat); 1956kJ (468 cal); 10.3g carbohydrate; 21.2g protein; 4.8g fibre

burmese clam and mussel stir-fry

preparation time 20 minutes (plus standing time) | cooking time 15 minutes | serves 4

500g large black mussels

500g clams

2 teaspoons shrimp paste

1 small red onion (100g), quartered

2 x 10cm sticks fresh lemon grass (40g),
    chopped finely

4 fresh kaffir lime leaves

2cm piece fresh galangal (10g), sliced thinly

2 tablespoons sambal oelek

1 tablespoon grated palm sugar

2 tablespoons peanut oil

¼ cup (60ml) lime juice

1 tablespoon cornflour

¼ cup (60ml) water

2 green onions, sliced thickly

1 fresh long red chilli, sliced thinly

1 Scrub mussels; remove beards.

2 Rinse clams under cold water; place in large bowl, sprinkle with salt, cover with water. Soak 1½ hours; rinse, drain.

3 Meanwhile, wrap shrimp paste securely in small piece of foil. Heat wok; stir-fry shrimp paste parcel until fragrant. Discard foil; blend or process shrimp paste with red onion, lemon grass, lime leaves, galangal, sambal and sugar until mixture forms a smooth paste.

4 Heat oil in wok; stir-fry paste 5 minutes. Add clams, mussels and juice; stir-fry 2 minutes. Cover wok; cook about 5 minutes or until clams and mussels open (discard any that do not).

5 Uncover wok, stir in blended cornflour and the water; stir-fry until sauce boils and thickens. Sprinkle with green onion and chilli.

per serving 10.5g total fat (1.8g saturated); 723kJ (173 cal); 12.2g carbohydrate; 6.9g protein; 0.9g fibre

goes well with steamed jasmine rice.

dry fish curry

preparation time 15 minutes | cooking time 25 minutes | serves 4

1 tablespoon peanut oil

⅓ cup (100g) green curry paste

2 tablespoons grated palm sugar

2 teaspoons fish sauce

¼ cup (60ml) lime juice

100g green beans, trimmed, halved crossways

⅔ cup (180ml) coconut cream

vegetable oil, for deep-frying

800g firm white fish fillets, cut into 3cm cubes

3 egg whites, beaten lightly

1 cup (200g) rice flour

2 tablespoons fried shallots

⅓ cup loosely packed thai basil leaves

1 Heat peanut oil in large frying pan; cook paste, stirring, until fragrant. Add sugar, sauce, juice, beans and coconut cream; bring to a boil. Remove from heat; cover curry sauce to keep warm.

2 Heat vegetable oil in wok. Dip fish in egg white then flour; shake off excess. Deep-fry fish, in batches, until browned; drain on absorbent paper.

3 Stir fish into curry sauce; serve sprinkled with shallots and basil.

per serving 37g total fat (12.6g saturated fat); 3127kJ (748 cal); 51.4g carbohydrate; 49.7g protein; 5.2g fibre

seafood and vegetable tempura

preparation time 35 minutes | cooking time 25 minutes | serves 6

540g uncooked medium king prawns

1 medium brown onion (150g)

peanut oil, for deep-frying

450g ocean trout fillets, cut into 3cm pieces

1 large red capsicum (350g), cut into 3cm pieces

1 small kumara (250g), sliced thinly

8 baby zucchini with flowers attached (160g),
  stamens removed

1 cup (150g) plain flour

1 lemon, cut into wedges

tempura batter

1 egg white

2 cups (500ml) cold soda water

1¼ cups (185g) plain flour

1¼ cups (185g) cornflour

lemon dipping sauce

½ cup (125ml) rice vinegar

¼ cup (55g) caster sugar

1 teaspoon light soy sauce

¼ teaspoon finely grated lemon rind

1 green onion (green part only), sliced thinly

1 Shell and devein prawns, leaving tails intact. Make three small cuts on the underside of each prawn, halfway through flesh, to prevent curling when cooked.

2 Halve onion from root end. Push 4 toothpicks, at regular intervals, through each onion half to hold rings together; cut in between toothpicks.

3 Make tempura batter. Make lemon dipping sauce.

4 Heat oil in wok. Dust prawns, onion, fish, capsicum, kumara and zucchini in flour; shake off excess. Dip, piece by piece, in batter; deep-fry until crisp. Drain on absorbent paper.

5 Serve tempura with dipping sauce and lemon wedges, if you like.

tempura batter Whisk egg white in large bowl until soft peaks form; add soda water, whisk to combine. Add sifted flours, whisk to combine (batter should be lumpy).

lemon dipping sauce Heat vinegar, sugar and sauce in small saucepan, stirring, until sugar dissolves. Remove from heat, add rind; stand 10 minutes. Strain sauce into serving dish; discard rind. Sprinkle sauce with onion.

per serving 16.6g total fat (3.1g saturated fat); 1831kJ (438 cal); 40.2g carbohydrate; 16.6g protein; 3.5g fibre

tip Only fry small batches of food at a time, making sure that the oil returns to correct temperature before adding next batch.

BABY ZUCCHINI *also known as courgette; small, pale- or dark-green, yellow or white vegetable belonging to the squash family. Harvested when young, its edible flowers can be stuffed and deep-fried or oven-baked to make a delicious appetiser.*

fish curry in lime and coconut

preparation time 25 minutes | cooking time 35 minutes | serves 4

6 fresh small red thai chillies, chopped coarsely
2 cloves garlic, quartered
10 shallots (250g), chopped coarsely
10cm stick fresh lemon grass (20g), chopped coarsely
5cm piece fresh galangal (25g), quartered
¼ cup coarsely chopped coriander root and
    stem mixture
¼ teaspoon ground turmeric
1 tablespoon peanut oil
2 x 400ml cans coconut milk
2 tablespoons fish sauce
4 fresh kaffir lime leaves, shredded
1 tablespoon lime juice
4 x 200g kingfish fillets
½ cup loosely packed fresh coriander leaves

1   Blend or process chilli, garlic, shallot, lemon grass, galangal, coriander root and stem mixture, turmeric and oil until mixture forms a smooth paste.

2   Cook paste in large frying pan, stirring, over medium heat, about 3 minutes or until fragrant. Add coconut milk, sauce and lime leaves; bring to a boil. Reduce heat; simmer, uncovered, about 15 minutes or until thickened slightly. Stir in juice.

3   Add fish to pan; simmer, uncovered, about 10 minutes or until cooked. Serve curry sprinkled with coriander leaves.

per serving 50.6g total fat (38.5g saturated fat); 2867kJ (686 cal); 10.6g carbohydrate; 45.9g protein; 4.9g fibre

goes well with steamed basmati rice.

tip We used kingfish in this curry, but you can replace it with any firm white fish with a meaty texture.

CORIANDER *also known as cilantro or chinese parsley; bright-green-leafed herb with a pungent flavour. Often stirred into or sprinkled over a dish just before serving for maximum impact. Both the stems and roots of coriander are also used in Thai cooking; wash well before chopping.*

poultry

shantung chicken

preparation time 10 minutes (plus refrigeration time) | cooking time 1 hour 20 minutes | serves 4

1 clove garlic, crushed

2cm piece fresh ginger (10g), grated

1 tablespoon dark soy sauce

1 tablespoon dry sherry

2 teaspoons sichuan peppercorns, crushed

2 teaspoons peanut oil

1.6kg whole chicken

shantung sauce

⅓ cup (75g) caster sugar

½ cup (125ml) water

2 tablespoons white wine vinegar

1 fresh small red thai chilli, chopped finely

1 Combine garlic, ginger, sauce, sherry, pepper and oil in large bowl; add chicken, coat in marinade. Cover; refrigerate overnight.

2 Preheat oven to 220°C/200°C fan-forced.

3 Half-fill a large baking dish with water; place chicken on oiled wire rack set over dish. Roast, uncovered, about 1 hour 20 minutes or until cooked through.

4 Meanwhile, make shantung sauce.

5 Remove chicken from oven; when cool enough to handle, remove bones. Chop meat coarsely; serve drizzled with sauce.

shantung sauce Combine sugar and the water in small saucepan; stir over low heat until sugar dissolves. Bring to a boil; boil, uncovered, without stirring, about 5 minutes or until sauce thickens slightly. Remove from heat; stir in vinegar and chilli.

per serving 28.3g total fat (8.6g saturated); 2107kJ (504 cal); 19.2g carbohydrate; 42.1g protein; 0.2g fibre

goes well with crisp fried noodles.

sake chicken

preparation time 10 minutes | cooking time 15 minutes | serves 4

*Japanese dry rice wine, sake, is also a basic ingredient in
many of the country's most well-known dishes. Special
and first-grade sake is sold for drinking while ryoriyo sake,
with its lower alcohol content, is made especially for use
in marinades, cooking and dipping sauces.*

800g chicken breast fillets
½ cup (125ml) cooking sake
1 clove garlic, crushed
1 fresh long red chilli, chopped finely
2 tablespoons rice vinegar
2 tablespoons japanese soy sauce
1 tablespoon lemon juice
2 teaspoons sesame oil
1 teaspoon caster sugar
2 green onions, sliced thinly
2 tablespoons pickled ginger, shredded finely

1   Combine chicken, sake, garlic, chilli, vinegar, sauce, juice,
oil and sugar in large frying pan; bring to a boil. Reduce heat;
simmer, covered, about 10 minutes or until chicken is cooked
through. Remove from heat; stand chicken in poaching liquid
10 minutes before slicing thickly. Cover to keep warm.

2   Bring poaching liquid to a boil; boil, uncovered, about
5 minutes or until sauce thickens. Serve chicken drizzled with
sauce, topped with onion and ginger.

per serving 13.4g total fat (3.7g saturated); 1413kJ (338cal);
2.9g carbohydrate; 43.6g protein; 0.4g fibre

goes well with steamed koshihikari rice.

PICKLED GINGER *pink or red coloured and
available from Asian food shops. Paper-thin
shavings of ginger that are pickled in a mixture
of vinegar, sugar and natural colouring; most
often used in Japanese cooking.*

spicy tamarind chicken

preparation time 10 minutes │ cooking time 1 hour │ serves 4

4 chicken marylands (1.5kg)
1 cup (250ml) water
¼ cup (85g) tamarind concentrate
¼ cup (60ml) japanese soy sauce
⅓ cup (90g) firmly packed grated palm sugar
chilli, ginger and lime paste
2 fresh small red thai chillies
5cm piece fresh ginger (25g), chopped coarsely
6 shallots (150g), chopped coarsely
2 cloves garlic
3 fresh kaffir lime leaves
1 tablespoon vegetable oil
1 tablespoon water

1   Make chilli, ginger and lime paste.

2   Preheat oven to 180°C/160°C fan-forced.

3   Heat oiled large shallow flameproof dish; cook chicken, uncovered, until browned, turning occasionally.

4   Remove chicken from dish. Cook paste, stirring, in same heated dish until fragrant. Stir in remaining ingredients then return chicken to dish, turning to coat in paste mixture.

5   Cook chicken, uncovered, in oven about 30 minutes or until cooked through, brushing frequently with paste mixture. Serve with lime wedges, if you like.

chilli, ginger and lime paste Blend or process ingredients until mixture forms a smooth paste.

per serving 39.6g total fat (11.8g saturated fat); 2713kJ (649 cal); 26.5g carbohydrate; 46.9g protein; 1.1g fibre

goes well with thin rice noodles.

thai basil chicken and snake bean stir-fry

preparation time 20 minutes (plus refrigeration time) │ cooking time 20 minutes │ serves 4

800g chicken thigh fillets, sliced thinly
¼ cup (60ml) fish sauce
1 tablespoon grated palm sugar
¼ teaspoon ground white pepper
1 tablespoon peanut oil
3 cloves garlic, sliced thinly
2cm piece fresh ginger (10g), sliced thinly
½ teaspoon dried chilli flakes
250g snake beans, cut into 5cm lengths
2 medium yellow capsicums (400g), sliced thinly
⅓ cup (80ml) chinese cooking wine
⅓ cup (80ml) lemon juice
1 tablespoon dark soy sauce
½ cup loosely packed thai basil leaves

1   Combine chicken, fish sauce, sugar and pepper in large bowl, cover; refrigerate 1 hour.

2   Heat oil in wok; stir-fry chicken mixture about 10 minutes or until almost cooked. Add garlic, ginger, chilli, beans and capsicum; stir-fry until beans are tender.

3   Add wine, juice and soy sauce; bring to a boil. Reduce heat; simmer, uncovered, 2 minutes. Remove from heat; stir in basil.

per serving 19.4g total fat (5.2g saturated fat); 1622kJ (388 cal); 8.6g carbohydrate; 42.4g protein; 3.3g fibre

goes well with fresh wide rice noodles.

coconut-poached chicken with thai-flavours salad

preparation time 30 minutes | cooking time 25 minutes | serves 4

2 x 400ml cans coconut milk

1 tablespoon coarsely chopped fresh coriander root and stem mixture

2 cloves garlic, sliced thinly

2 fresh kaffir lime leaves, shredded finely

800g chicken breast fillets

10cm stick fresh lemon grass (20g)

1 lebanese cucumber (130g), halved lengthways, seeded, sliced thinly

1½ cups (120g) bean sprouts

¾ cup loosely packed fresh coriander leaves

½ cup loosely packed fresh mint leaves

1 fresh long red chilli, sliced thinly

coriander and lime dressing

2 teaspoons coarsely chopped fresh coriander root and stem mixture

2 cloves garlic, peeled

2 fresh small red thai chillies

1 tablespoon caster sugar

¼ cup (60ml) lime juice

2 teaspoons fish sauce

1 Combine coconut milk, coriander root and stem mixture, garlic and lime leaves in large saucepan; bring to a boil. Add chicken; return to a boil. Reduce heat; simmer, uncovered, about 10 minutes or until cooked through. Remove from heat; stand chicken in poaching liquid 10 minutes. Remove chicken from pan; when cool enough to handle, shred coarsely.

2 Reserve 1 cup poaching liquid; discard remainder. Bring reserved liquid to a boil in same pan; boil, uncovered, about 10 minutes or until reduced by two-thirds. Add chicken to pan with liquid; cool 10 minutes.

3 Meanwhile, make coriander and lime dressing.

4 Soak lemon grass in small heatproof bowl covered with boiling water about 4 minutes or until just tender; drain. Slice thinly; combine in large bowl with cucumber, sprouts, coriander leaves, mint, chilli and dressing. Divide chicken mixture among serving plates; top with salad.

coriander and lime dressing Using mortar and pestle, crush coriander root and stem mixture, garlic, chillies and sugar until combined. Gradually add juice; crush until sugar dissolves. Stir in fish sauce.

per serving 52.7g total fat (39.7g saturated fat); 3056kJ (731 cal); 13.9g carbohydrate; 48.7g protein; 6g fibre

grilled chicken with coriander and chilli

preparation time 10 minutes (plus refrigeration time) | cooking time 25 minutes | serves 4

8 chicken thigh cutlets (1.6kg)

coriander and chilli paste

2 teaspoons coriander seeds

4 fresh small red thai chillies, chopped coarsely

1 teaspoon ground cumin

2 whole cloves

2 cardamom pods, bruised

¼ teaspoon ground turmeric

10cm stick fresh lemon grass (20g), chopped coarsely

2 medium brown onions (300g), chopped coarsely

4 cloves garlic

⅓ cup (80ml) lime juice

2 teaspoons coarse cooking salt

2 tablespoons peanut oil

1   Make coriander and chilli paste.

2   Pierce chicken all over with sharp knife. Combine paste and chicken in large bowl, rubbing paste into cuts. Cover; refrigerate overnight.

3   Cook chicken, covered, on heated oiled grill plate (or grill or barbecue), 5 minutes. Uncover; cook, turning occasionally, about 20 minutes or until cooked. Serve with lime wedges, if you like.

coriander and chilli paste Blend or process ingredients until mixture forms a smooth paste.

per serving 29.5g total fat (7.8g saturated fat); 2094kJ (501 cal); 5.2g carbohydrate; 53.5g protein; 1.7g fibre

goes well with thin rice noodles.

crisp duck with mandarin, chilli and mint

preparation time 25 minutes | cooking time 30 minutes | serves 4

You need about six small mandarins in total for this recipe: two for the rind and segments, and four for the required amount of juice.

2 small mandarins (200g)

½ cup (135g) firmly packed grated palm sugar

½ cup (125ml) water

⅓ cup (80ml) mandarin juice

1 tablespoon lime juice

2 teaspoons fish sauce

1 fresh long red chilli, chopped finely

1 star anise

2 tablespoons plain flour

2 teaspoons sea salt flakes

1 teaspoon dried chilli flakes

4 duck breast fillets (600g)

4 green onions, sliced thinly

½ cup loosely packed fresh mint leaves

1 fresh long red chilli, sliced thinly

1   Using vegetable peeler, cut four 5cm-strips of peel from mandarins. Remove remaining peel and pith; discard. Segment mandarins into small heatproof bowl.

2   Combine peel, sugar and the water in small saucepan. Stir over low heat until sugar dissolves; bring to a boil. Reduce heat; simmer, uncovered, without stirring, about 10 minutes or until syrup thickens slightly. Add juices, sauce, chopped chilli and star anise to pan; bring to a boil. Reduce heat; simmer, uncovered, about 5 minutes or until thickened slightly. Discard star anise; pour dressing into bowl with mandarin segments. Cool.

3   Meanwhile, combine flour, salt and dried chilli in medium bowl. Coat duck fillets, one at a time, in flour mixture; shake off excess. Cook duck, skin-side down, in heated oiled large frying pan, over medium heat, about 10 minutes or until crisp. Turn duck; cook about 5 minutes or until cooked as desired. Remove from heat; slice thickly.

4   Divide duck and mandarin segments among serving plates; top with onion, mint and sliced chilli, drizzle with dressing.

per serving 55.6g total fat (16.7g saturated fat); 3148kJ (753 cal); 42.3g carbohydrate; 21.2g protein; 1.7g fibre

pistachio chicken

preparation time 15 minutes (plus refrigeration time) | cooking time 30 minutes | serves 4

1kg chicken thigh fillets, cut into 3cm pieces

1⅓ cups (400g) yogurt

2 teaspoons peanut oil

¼ cup coarsely chopped fresh coriander

¼ cup (35g) coarsely chopped roasted
    unsalted pistachios

pistachio paste

¾ cup (105g) roasted unsalted pistachios

1 medium brown onion (150g), chopped coarsely

⅓ cup (95g) yogurt

2 tablespoons peanut oil

2 cloves garlic, quartered

1 long green chilli, chopped coarsely

1 tablespoon lemon juice

1 teaspoon ground coriander

1 teaspoon ground cumin

½ teaspoon ground cardamom

1   Make pistachio paste.

2   Combine chicken, yogurt and ½ cup of the paste in medium bowl, cover; refrigerate 30 minutes.

3   Heat oil in large saucepan; cook remaining paste, stirring, until fragrant. Add chicken mixture; bring to a boil. Reduce heat; simmer, covered, about 20 minutes or until chicken is cooked through.

4   Sprinkle chicken with coriander and nuts.

pistachio paste Blend or process ingredients until mixture forms a smooth paste.

per serving 51.4g total fat (12.3g saturated fat); 3173kJ (759 cal); 13.5g carbohydrate; 60g protein; 4g fibre

goes well with steamed basmati rice.

tamarind, lime and honey chicken salad

preparation time 35 minutes (plus refrigeration time) | cooking time 20 minutes | serves 4

¼ cup (60ml) peanut oil

¼ cup (60ml) tamarind concentrate

1 tablespoon honey

2 teaspoons dark soy sauce

½ teaspoon finely grated lime rind

1 tablespoon lime juice

1 clove garlic, crushed

800g chicken breast fillets

½ small wombok (350g), trimmed, shredded finely

4 green onions, sliced thinly

500g red radishes, trimmed, sliced thinly,
    cut into matchsticks

2 lebanese cucumbers (260g), halved widthways,
    seeded, cut into matchsticks

½ cup loosely packed fresh mint leaves

½ cup loosely packed fresh coriander leaves

⅔ cup (50g) fried shallots

honey lime dressing

1 tablespoon honey

2 tablespoons lime juice

1 teaspoon sesame oil

1 tablespoon dark soy sauce

1 fresh long red chilli, chopped finely

1   Combine 1 tablespoon of the oil, tamarind, honey, sauce, rind, juice, garlic and chicken in large bowl, cover; refrigerate 3 hours or overnight.

2   Make honey lime dressing.

3   Heat remaining oil in large frying pan; cook chicken mixture, in batches, until cooked through. Stand 5 minutes; slice chicken thickly. Cover to keep warm.

4   Meanwhile, combine dressing in large bowl with remaining ingredients. Divide salad among plates; top with chicken.

honey lime dressing Combine ingredients in screw-top jar; shake well.

per serving 27g total fat (6.1g saturated fat); 2144kJ (513 cal); 19.4g carbohydrate; 46.3g protein; 4.3g fibre

TAMARIND *although generally associated with the food of India and South-East Asia, is actually from a native tropical African tree. The tree produces clusters of brown "hairy" pods, each of which is filled with seeds and a viscous pulp that are dried and pressed into the blocks of tamarind found in Asian supermarkets. Dried tamarind is reconstituted in a hot liquid that gives a sweet-sour, astringent taste to food. The pulp is also commercially produced as a concentrate, which makes it easy for the home cook to use; this can be kept in the refrigerator indefinitely. Tamarind is also used as a souring agent in commercial marinades, pastes, sauces and dressings.*

white-cut chicken

preparation time 20 minutes (plus standing time) | cooking time 45 minutes | serves 4

1.6kg whole chicken
2 litres (8 cups) water
¼ cup (60ml) light soy sauce
½ cup (125ml) dark soy sauce
1 cup (250ml) chinese cooking wine
½ cup (135g) coarsely chopped palm sugar
20cm piece fresh ginger (100g), sliced thinly
4 star anise
4 cloves garlic, sliced thinly
1 tablespoon sichuan peppercorns
soy and green onion dressing
¼ cup (60ml) dark soy sauce
¼ cup (60ml) rice vinegar
4 green onions, sliced thinly
2 teaspoons peanut oil
½ teaspoon sesame oil

1   Make soy and green onion dressing.

2   Place chicken, breast-side down with remaining ingredients in large saucepan; bring to a boil. Reduce heat; simmer, uncovered, 25 minutes. Turn chicken breast-side up; simmer, uncovered, 5 minutes. Remove pan from heat; turn chicken breast-side down, stand in poaching liquid 3 hours.

3   Remove chicken from pan; discard poaching liquid. Using cleaver, cut chicken in half through the centre of the breastbone and along one side of backbone; cut each half into eight pieces. Serve chicken drizzled with dressing.

soy and green onion dressing Whisk ingredients in small bowl.

per serving 26.2g total fat (8.7g saturated fat); 2621kJ (627 cal); 41.3g carbohydrate; 46.3g protein; 1.2g fibre

goes well with steamed jasmine rice and asian greens.

CHINESE COOKING WINE is made from rice, wheat, sugar and salt, and has a 13.5% alcohol content. It is available from Asian food stores. Mirin or sherry can be substituted, if preferred.

meat

twice-fried sichuan beef with buk choy

preparation time 20 minutes | cooking time 25 minutes | serves 4

½ cup (75g) cornflour
1 tablespoon sichuan peppercorns, crushed coarsely
600g piece beef eye fillet, sliced thinly
vegetable oil, for deep-frying
2 teaspoons sesame oil
1 clove garlic, crushed
2 fresh small red thai chillies, chopped finely
1 medium brown onion (150g), sliced thinly
1 medium carrot (120g), halved, sliced thinly
1 medium red capsicum (200g), sliced thinly
150g sugar snap peas, trimmed
300g baby buk choy, leaves separated
2 tablespoons oyster sauce
¼ cup (60ml) japanese soy sauce
¼ cup (60ml) beef stock
2 tablespoons dry sherry
1 tablespoon brown sugar

1   Combine cornflour and half the pepper in medium bowl with beef.

2   Heat vegetable oil in wok; deep-fry beef, in batches, until crisp. Drain on absorbent paper.

3   Heat sesame oil in cleaned wok; stir-fry garlic, chilli and onion until onion softens. Add carrot and capsicum; stir-fry until vegetables soften.

4   Return beef to wok with remaining ingredients; stir-fry until buk choy is wilted.

per serving 19.5g total fat (5.1g saturated); 1914kJ (458cal); 29.6g carbohydrate; 36.4g protein; 3.8g fibre
goes well with steamed jasmine rice.

tip | This recipe can be prepared, up to step 5, the day before serving.

crisp pork belly with wombok salad

preparation time 50 minutes (plus refrigeration time) | cooking time 2 hours 15 minutes | serves 4

2 cups (500ml) salt-reduced chicken stock

⅓ cup (80ml) chinese cooking wine

½ cup (125ml) lime juice

¼ cup (60ml) japanese soy sauce

2 dried red chillies

2 star anise

1 tablespoon coarsely chopped fresh coriander root
    and stem mixture

2cm piece fresh ginger (10g), sliced thinly

2 cloves garlic, halved

2 fresh kaffir lime leaves, torn

800g piece pork belly

¼ cup (60ml) oyster sauce

⅓ cup (90g) firmly packed grated palm sugar

2 tablespoons fish sauce

1 tablespoon peanut oil

2 fresh long red chillies, chopped finely

2cm piece fresh ginger (10g), grated

1 clove garlic, crushed

½ medium wombok (500g), shredded finely

1 medium red capsicum (200g), sliced thinly

1 large carrot (180g), sliced thinly

1 cup (80g) bean sprouts

2 green onions, sliced thinly

½ cup loosely packed fresh coriander leaves

½ cup loosely packed vietnamese mint leaves

½ cup (70g) roasted unsalted peanuts,
    chopped coarsely

¼ cup (20g) fried shallots

1 Combine stock, wine, half the juice, soy sauce, dried chillies, star anise, coriander root and stem mixture, sliced ginger, halved garlic, lime leaves and pork in large deep flameproof dish; bring to a boil. Reduce heat; simmer, covered tightly, about 1½ hours or until pork is tender.

2 Remove pork from dish. Strain broth through muslin-lined sieve into medium saucepan; discard solids. Bring broth to a boil; boil, uncovered, 10 minutes.

3 Slice pork lengthways into 1cm-thick slices. Combine pork with half the broth and oyster sauce in large bowl. Cover; refrigerate 2 hours.

4 Meanwhile, to make dressing, stir sugar into remaining broth; bring to a boil, stirring until sugar dissolves. Reduce heat; simmer, uncovered, about 5 minutes or until thickened slightly. Remove from heat; stir in remaining juice, fish sauce, oil, fresh chilli, grated ginger and crushed garlic. Cool dressing.

5 Preheat oven to 240°C/220°C fan-forced. Oil two oven trays, line with baking paper.

6 Drain pork; discard marinade. Place pork, in single layer, on trays; cook, uncovered, turning occasionally, about 20 minutes or until crisp. Cut pork slices into 2cm pieces.

7 Meanwhile, place wombok, capsicum, carrot, sprouts, onion, coriander leaves, mint, nuts and dressing in large bowl; add pork, toss gently to combine.

8 Divide salad among serving bowls, sprinkle with shallots.

per serving 58.7g total fat (17.6g saturated fat); 4009kJ (959 cal); 37.7g carbohydrate; 64.8g protein; 16.8g fibre

lamb and macadamia curry

preparation time 20 minutes | cooking time 2 hours 20 minutes | serves 4

1 cup (140g) roasted unsalted macadamias
2 tablespoons vegetable oil
800g diced lamb shoulder
1 medium brown onion (150g), chopped coarsely
1 clove garlic, crushed
2 fresh small red thai chillies, chopped finely
2cm piece fresh ginger (10g), grated
1 teaspoon ground cumin
1 teaspoon ground turmeric
½ teaspoon ground cinnamon
½ teaspoon ground cardamom
½ teaspoon ground fennel
400g can diced tomatoes
400ml can coconut milk
1 cup (250ml) beef stock
½ cup loosely packed fresh coriander leaves

1   Blend or process half the nuts until finely ground; coarsely chop remaining nuts.

2   Heat half the oil in large saucepan; cook lamb, in batches, until browned.

3   Heat remaining oil in same pan; cook onion, garlic, chilli and ginger, stirring, until onion softens. Add spices; cook, stirring, until fragrant. Return lamb to pan with ground nuts, undrained tomatoes, coconut milk and stock; bring to a boil. Reduce heat; simmer, covered, about 1¼ hours or until lamb is tender. Uncover; simmer about 15 minutes or until sauce thickens slightly.

4   Serve lamb sprinkled with remaining nuts and coriander.

per serving 68.4g total fat (28.4g saturated); 3561kJ (852cal); 11.6g carbohydrate; 47g protein; 5.9g fibre
goes well with steamed basmati rice.

plum and star anise pork spareribs with pear, ginger and chilli salad

preparation time 25 minutes (plus refrigeration time) | cooking time 30 minutes | serves 4

2kg slabs american-style pork spareribs

plum and star anise marinade

1 cup (250ml) plum sauce

5cm piece fresh ginger (25g), grated

⅓ cup (80ml) oyster sauce

2 star anise

1 teaspoon dried chilli flakes

pear, ginger and chilli salad

2 medium pears (460g), sliced thinly

2 fresh long red chillies, sliced thinly

2 green onions, sliced thinly

2 cups coarsely chopped fresh mint

2cm piece fresh ginger (10g), grated

2 tablespoons lime juice

1 Make plum and star anise marinade.

2 Place pork in large shallow baking dish; brush marinade all over pork. Pour remaining marinade over pork, cover; refrigerate 3 hours or overnight, turning pork occasionally.

3 Drain pork; reserve marinade. Cook pork on heated oiled grill plate (or grill or barbecue) about 30 minutes or until cooked through, turning and brushing frequently with some of the reserved marinade.

4 Meanwhile, make pear, ginger and chilli salad.

5 Boil remaining marinade, uncovered, in small saucepan about 5 minutes or until thickened slightly.

6 Slice slabs into portions; serve with hot marinade and salad.

plum and star anise marinade Combine ingredients in medium saucepan; bring to a boil. Remove from heat; cool 10 minutes.

pear, ginger and chilli salad Combine ingredients in medium bowl.

per serving 18.1g total fat (6.6g saturated fat); 2847kJ (681 cal); 56.3g carbohydrate; 69.6g protein; 5.2g fibre

STAR ANISE *is a dried star-shaped pod whose seeds have an astringent aniseed flavour; it is used to flavour stocks and marinades.*

lamb shanks massaman

preparation time 30 minutes | cooking time 2 hours 30 minutes | serves 4

Having a spicy flavour reminiscent of many Indian or Pakistani dishes, Thai massaman curries evolved from foods originally introduced by Muslim traders from India and Pakistan. Massaman paste remains a favourite of the Muslim communities in southern Thailand for use in hot and sour stew-like curries and sauces.

1 tablespoon vegetable oil

8 french trimmed lamb shanks (2kg)

2 large brown onions (400g), chopped coarsely

400ml can coconut milk

2 tablespoons tamarind concentrate

2 cups (500ml) beef stock

700g piece pumpkin, trimmed, cut into 2cm cubes

¼ cup (35g) roasted unsalted peanuts,
    chopped coarsely

2 green onions, sliced thinly

massaman curry paste

20 dried red chillies

1 teaspoon ground coriander

2 teaspoons ground cumin

2 teaspoons ground cinnamon

½ teaspoon ground cardamom

½ teaspoon ground clove

5 cloves garlic, quartered

1 large brown onion (200g), chopped coarsely

2 x 10cm sticks fresh lemon grass (40g), sliced thinly

3 fresh kaffir lime leaves, sliced thinly

4cm piece fresh ginger (20g), chopped coarsely

2 teaspoons shrimp paste

1 tablespoon peanut oil

1   Preheat oven to 180°C/160°C fan-forced.

2   Make massaman curry paste.

3   Heat half the oil in large flameproof dish; cook lamb, in batches, until browned.

4   Heat remaining oil in same dish; cook brown onion and ½ cup curry paste, stirring, 2 minutes. Add coconut milk, tamarind and stock; bring to a boil. Remove from heat, add lamb; cook in oven, covered, 2 hours. Remove lamb from dish; cover.

5   Add pumpkin to dish; bring to a boil. Reduce heat; simmer, uncovered, about 10 minutes or until pumpkin is tender and sauce is thickened.

6   Divide lamb, pumpkin and sauce among serving plates, sprinkle with nuts and green onion.

massaman curry paste   Place chillies in small heatproof jug, cover with boiling water, stand 15 minutes; drain, reserve chillies. Meanwhile, dry-fry coriander, cumin, cinnamon, cardamom and clove in small frying pan, stirring, until fragrant. Place chillies and roasted spices in small shallow baking dish with remaining ingredients. Roast, uncovered, in oven 15 minutes. Blend or process roasted mixture until smooth. Freeze the remaining curry paste, covered, after you use the ½ cup called for in this recipe.

per serving   57.2g total fat (31.4g saturated fat); 3628kJ (868 cal); 20.7g carbohydrate; 65.7g protein; 6g fibre

stir-fried pork, buk choy and water chestnuts

preparation time 15 minutes (plus refrigeration time) | cooking time 15 minutes | serves 4

¼ cup (60ml) light soy sauce

2 tablespoons oyster sauce

1 tablespoon honey

1 tablespoon chinese cooking wine

1 teaspoon five-spice powder

½ teaspoon sesame oil

1 clove garlic, crushed

600g pork fillets, sliced thinly

2 tablespoons peanut oil

600g baby buk choy, chopped coarsely

227g can water chestnuts, rinsed, drained,
    sliced thickly

½ cup (75g) unsalted roasted cashews

2 long green chillies, sliced thinly

1 tablespoon water

1 Combine 2 tablespoons of the soy sauce, 1 tablespoon of the oyster sauce, honey, wine, five-spice, sesame oil, garlic and pork in large bowl. Cover; refrigerate 3 hours or overnight.

2 Stir-fry pork in oiled wok, in batches, until browned.

3 Heat peanut oil in same wok; stir-fry buk choy, water chestnuts, nuts and chilli until tender.

4 Return pork to wok with remaining soy and oyster sauces and the water; stir-fry until hot.

per serving 23g total fat (4.5g saturated fat); 1827kJ (437 cal); 15.8g carbohydrate; 39.1g protein; 4.1g fibre

braised beef brisket

preparation time 20 minutes | cooking time 2 hours | serves 4

2 tablespoons vegetable oil

1kg beef brisket, trimmed, cut into 3cm pieces

1 small brown onion (80g), sliced thinly

2 cloves garlic, crushed

2cm piece fresh ginger (10g), grated

2 tablespoons fish sauce

1 tablespoon dark soy sauce

1 tablespoon brown sugar

1 teaspoon five-spice powder

2 x 10cm sticks fresh lemon grass (40g),
    halved crossways

2 cups (500ml) water

150g snake beans, chopped coarsely

¾ cup (105g) crushed peanuts

⅓ cup loosely packed vietnamese mint leaves

1 Heat half the oil in large saucepan; cook beef, in batches, until browned lightly.

2 Heat remaining oil in same pan; cook onion, garlic and ginger until onion softens.

3 Return beef to pan with sauces, sugar, five-spice, lemon grass and the water; bring to a boil. Reduce heat; simmer, covered, about 1¼ hours or until beef is tender. Discard lemon grass. Add beans and ½ cup of the nuts; simmer, uncovered, 15 minutes.

4 Serve beef, sprinkled with remaining nuts and mint.

per serving 35.6g total fat (8.3g saturated); 2458kJ (588 cal); 8.3g carbohydrate; 56.8g protein; 4.2g fibre
goes well with steamed jasmine rice.

chilli-garlic mince with snake beans

preparation time 10 minutes | cooking time 15 minutes | serves 4

2 cloves garlic, quartered

2 long green chillies, chopped coarsely

2 fresh small red thai chillies, chopped coarsely

1 tablespoon peanut oil

600g beef mince

150g snake beans, chopped coarsely

1 medium red capsicum (200g), sliced thinly

2 tablespoons kecap asin

¼ cup (60ml) hoisin sauce

4 green onions, sliced thickly

2 tablespoons crushed peanuts

1   Blend or process garlic and chilli until mixture is finely chopped.

2   Heat half the oil in wok; stir-fry garlic mixture until fragrant. Add beef; stir-fry, in batches, until cooked through.

3   Heat remaining oil in cleaned wok; stir-fry beans and capsicum until tender.

4   Return beef to wok with sauces and onion; stir-fry until hot. Sprinkle over nuts; serve with lime wedges, if you like.

per serving 18.6g total fat (5.6g saturated fat); 1476kJ (353 cal); 9.6g carbohydrate; 34.8g protein; 4.2g fibre

SNAKE BEANS *long (about 40cm), thin, round, fresh green beans; Asian in origin with a taste similar to green or french beans. Used most frequently in stir-fries, they are also called yard-long beans because of their (pre-metric) length.*

tonkatsu-don

preparation time 25 minutes | cooking time 30 minutes | serves 4

We used koshihikari rice in this recipe, but you can also use arborio rice if it's more readily available.

Prepared tonkatsu sauce is sold in most supermarkets and Asian food stores if you don't wish to make your own.

3 cups (750ml) water
1½ cups (300g) koshihikari rice
4 pork steaks (600g)
¼ cup (35g) plain flour
2 eggs
2 teaspoons water, extra
2 cups (100g) japanese breadcrumbs
1 tablespoon peanut oil
2 cloves garlic, sliced thinly
½ small wombok (350g), shredded finely
1 fresh small red thai chilli, chopped finely
1 tablespoon mirin
1 tablespoon light soy sauce
vegetable oil, for deep-frying
2 green onions, sliced thinly

tonkatsu sauce

⅓ cup (80ml) tomato sauce
2 tablespoons japanese worcestershire sauce
2 tablespoons cooking sake
1 teaspoon japanese soy sauce
1 teaspoon japanese mustard

1 Make tonkatsu sauce.

2 Combine the water and rice in medium saucepan; bring to a boil. Reduce heat; cook, covered tightly, over very low heat, about 15 minutes or until water is absorbed. Remove from heat; stand, covered, 10 minutes.

3 Meanwhile, pound pork gently with meat mallet; coat in flour, shake off excess. Dip pork in combined egg and extra water then coat in breadcrumbs.

4 Heat peanut oil in wok; cook garlic, stirring, until fragrant. Add wombok and chilli; cook, stirring, 1 minute. Transfer wombok mixture to large bowl with mirin and sauce; toss to combine. Cover to keep warm.

5 Heat vegetable oil in cleaned wok; deep-fry pork, in batches, turning occasionally, about 5 minutes or until golden brown. Drain on absorbent paper. Cut pork diagonally into 2cm slices.

6 Divide rice among serving bowls; top with pork, wombok mixture then onion, drizzle with tonkatsu sauce.

tonkatsu sauce Combine ingredients in small saucepan; bring to a boil. Remove from heat; cool.

per serving 31.6g total fat (8g saturated fat); 3595kJ (860 cal); 91g carbohydrate; 46.7g protein; 4g fibre

tip | Japanese breadcrumbs, also known as panko, are available from Asian grocers and some supermarkets. If you can't find the Japanese variety, use stale breadcrumbs, instead.

lamb meatball korma

preparation time 45 minutes (plus standing time) | cooking time 1 hour 10 minutes | serves 4

½ cup (40g) desiccated coconut
⅓ cup (80ml) hot water
¼ cup (40g) unsalted roasted cashews
500g lamb mince
1 large brown onion (200g), chopped finely
½ cup (35g) stale breadcrumbs
1 egg
2 tablespoons ghee
2 bay leaves
1 cinnamon stick
5 cardamom pods, bruised
5 cloves
1 medium red onion (170g), sliced thinly
2cm piece fresh ginger (10g), grated
2 cloves garlic, crushed
½ teaspoon chilli powder
½ teaspoon ground turmeric
1 teaspoon ground coriander
½ teaspoon ground cumin
2 medium tomatoes (300g), chopped coarsely
1½ cups (375ml) water, extra
¾ cup (180ml) cream

1   Place coconut in small heatproof bowl, cover with the hot water; stand 1 hour, drain. Blend or process coconut and nuts until mixture forms a thick puree.

2   Mix 2 tablespoons of the coconut mixture, lamb, brown onion, breadcrumbs and egg in medium bowl; roll level tablespoons of mixture into balls.

3   Melt half the ghee in large saucepan; cook meatballs, in batches, until browned lightly. Drain on absorbent paper.

4   Heat remaining ghee in same cleaned pan; add leaves, cinnamon, cardamom and cloves. Cook, stirring, until fragrant. Add red onion; cook, stirring, until browned lightly. Add ginger, garlic, chilli, turmeric, coriander and cumin; cook, stirring, 1 minute. Add tomato; cook, stirring, about 5 minutes or until mixture thickens slightly. Add remaining coconut mixture and extra water; simmer, uncovered, 20 minutes.

5   Return meatballs to pan; simmer, covered, about 20 minutes or until cooked through. Stir in cream; simmer, stirring, until hot.

per serving 50.1g total fat (29.1g saturated fat); 2755kJ (659 cal); 17g carbohydrate; 34g protein; 5.5g fibre

goes well with steamed basmati rice.

beef carpaccio with green papaya salad

preparation 30 minutes (plus freezing time) | serves 4

Green (unripe) papaya has more crunch than flavour, and it acts as a sponge to absorb the combined hot, sour, sweet and salty Thai flavours of the salad.
You need a small fresh coconut for this recipe. See page 30 for the method to prepare fresh coconut.

600g piece beef eye fillet, trimmed
⅓ cup (35g) coarsely grated fresh coconut

green papaya salad
1 small green papaya (650g)
2 purple shallots (50g), sliced thinly
1 fresh long red chilli, chopped finely
¼ cup coarsely chopped fresh coriander
¼ cup coarsely chopped fresh mint
¼ cup (60ml) lime juice
1 tablespoon fish sauce
1 tablespoon grated palm sugar
1 tablespoon peanut oil

1   Wrap beef tightly in plastic wrap; place in freezer about 1 hour or until partially frozen. Unwrap beef; using sharp knife, slice beef as thinly as possible.

2   Make green papaya salad.

3   Arrange carpaccio in single layer on serving plates; top with salad, sprinkle with coconut.

green papaya salad Peel papaya, halve lengthways, remove seeds then grate coarsely into large bowl. Add remaining ingredients; toss to combine.

per serving 16.2g total fat (6.7g saturated); 1400kJ (335 cal); 12.2g carbohydrate; 33.2g protein; 3.8g fibre

GREEN PAPAYA *are available at Asian food stores; look for one that is hard and slightly shiny, proving it is freshly picked. Papaya will soften rapidly if not used within a day or two.*

vegetables

spicy carrot and zucchini bhaji

preparation time 15 minutes | cooking time 15 minutes | makes 20

The bustling streets of Indian cities are lined with many food stalls that sell a wide array of snacks, one of the most more-ish being bhaji, one or more vegetables grated, dredged in besan (chickpea) flour and deep-fried into fritter-like bites.

Grated zucchini can release a lot of water; if bhaji batter becomes runny, add enough besan flour to restore the batter to its original consistency.

1 cup (150g) besan flour
2 teaspoons coarse cooking salt
½ cup (125ml) cold water
¼ teaspoon ground turmeric
1 teaspoon chilli powder
1 teaspoon garam masala
2 cloves garlic, crushed
2 small brown onions (160g), sliced thinly
1 medium carrot (120g), grated coarsely
1 medium zucchini (120g), grated coarsely
½ cup loosely packed fresh coriander leaves
vegetable oil, for deep-frying
1 cup (320g) mango chutney

1   Whisk besan, salt and the water in medium bowl until mixture forms a smooth thick batter. Stir in spices, garlic, onion, carrot, zucchini and coriander.

2   Heat oil in wok; deep-fry tablespoons of mixture, in batches, until vegetables are tender and bhaji are browned lightly. Drain on absorbent paper. Serve with chutney.

per bhaji 2.3g total fat (0.3g saturated fat); 330kJ (79 cal); 12.1g carbohydrate; 2g protein; 1.6g fibre

sichuan eggplant, almond and wombok stir-fry

preparation time 15 minutes | cooking time 20 minutes | serves 4

⅓ cup (55g) blanched almonds, halved

1 tablespoon peanut oil

1 medium brown onion (150g), chopped coarsely

2 cloves garlic, crushed

1 fresh small red thai chilli, chopped finely

12 baby eggplants (720g), sliced thickly

150g snake beans, trimmed, chopped coarsely

1 small wombok (700g), trimmed, chopped coarsely

2 teaspoons sichuan peppercorns, crushed coarsely

¼ cup (60ml) vegetable stock

2 tablespoons hoisin sauce

1 tablespoon dark soy sauce

1 tablespoon red wine vinegar

½ cup loosely packed thai basil leaves

1 fresh long red chilli, sliced thinly

1   Stir-fry nuts in heated wok until browned lightly; remove from wok.

2   Heat oil in wok; stir-fry onion, garlic and thai chilli until onion softens. Add eggplant and beans; stir-fry until tender. Add wombok; stir-fry until wilted.

3   Add pepper, stock, sauces and vinegar; stir-fry until hot. Remove from heat; stir in basil. Serve sprinkled with nuts and chilli.

per serving 13.6g total fat (1.4g saturated); 982kJ (235cal); 13.9g carbohydrate; 9.3g protein; 10.7g fibre

goes well with stir-fried hokkien noodles.

spinach and mushroom korma

preparation time 15 minutes | cooking time 25 minutes | serves 4

⅓ cup (50g) unsalted roasted cashews

1 tablespoon ghee

1 large brown onion (200g), sliced thinly

2 cloves garlic, crushed

4cm piece fresh ginger (20g), grated

2 teaspoons kalonji seeds

½ cup (160g) prepared korma paste

⅔ cup (160ml) cream

400g swiss brown mushrooms

500g spinach, trimmed, chopped coarsely

⅓ cup (95g) yogurt

1   Blend or process nuts until finely ground.

2   Heat ghee in large saucepan; cook onion, garlic and ginger, stirring, until onion softens. Add nuts, seeds and paste; cook, stirring, until fragrant.

3   Add cream and mushrooms; simmer, covered, 15 minutes. Add spinach; cook, stirring, until wilted. Serve curry with yogurt.

per serving 41.8g total fat (17.2g saturated fat); 2065kJ (495 cal); 11.6g carbohydrate; 13.6g protein; 11.8g fibre

tip | For a non-vegetarian version of this salad, you can add cooked prawns or shredded chicken, if you like. Assemble the salad just before you want to serve it.

green papaya salad

preparation time 20 minutes (plus standing time) | serves 4

You need a small fresh coconut for this recipe. See page 30 for the method to prepare fresh coconut.

10cm stick fresh lemon grass (20g)
1 small green papaya (650g)
2 cups (160g) bean sprouts
1 cup (100g) coarsely grated fresh coconut
¾ cup loosely packed fresh coriander leaves
¾ cup loosely packed fresh mint leaves
2 purple shallots (50g), sliced thinly
½ cup (70g) roasted unsalted peanuts, chopped coarsely

chilli citrus dressing
¼ cup (60ml) lime juice
¼ cup (60ml) lemon juice
1 tablespoon grated palm sugar
2 teaspoons fish sauce
1 fresh small red thai chilli, chopped finely

1   Soak lemon grass in medium heatproof bowl of boiling water about 4 minutes or until tender. Drain; slice lemon grass thinly.

2   Meanwhile, make chilli citrus dressing.

3   Peel papaya, quarter lengthways, discard seeds; grate papaya coarsely.

4   Combine lemon grass, dressing, papaya, sprouts, coconut, coriander, mint and shallot in large bowl. Divide salad among serving bowls then sprinkle with nuts.

chilli citrus dressing Combine ingredients in screw-top jar; shake well.

per serving 15.5g total fat (7.3g saturated fat); 1049kJ (251 cal); 16.3g carbohydrate; 7.9g protein; 8.4g fibre

chillies filled with potato masala

preparation time 20 minutes | cooking time 1 hour 20 minutes | serves 4

In Indian cooking terms, masala literally means ground or blended spices but, informally, has come to mean a "mix" or "mixture"; a masala can be whole or ground spices, a paste or powder, or a sauce-like curry incorporating solid elements. Banana chillies, also known as wax chillies or hungarian peppers, are almost as mild as capsicum, but have a distinctively sweet sharpness to their taste. Sold in varying degrees of ripeness, they can be found in pale olive green, yellow and red varieties at greengrocers everywhere.
A popular unleavened Indian bread, similar in appearance to pitta only thinner, chapatis accompany saucy curries, often serving as cutlery to scoop up the food. They are available in the bread department of most supermarkets, delicatessens and Asian food stores.

500g potatoes, chopped coarsely
1 tablespoon vegetable oil
1 clove garlic, crushed
1 medium brown onion (150g), sliced thinly
½ teaspoon yellow mustard seeds
1 teaspoon garam masala
1 teaspoon ground coriander
½ teaspoon ground cumin
½ teaspoon chilli powder
¼ teaspoon ground turmeric
400g can chopped tomatoes
2 tablespoons sultanas
4 banana chillies (500g)
1 lebanese cucumber (130g), seeded, chopped finely
¾ cup (200g) greek-style yogurt
6 chapatis (280g), warmed

1 Preheat oven to 180°C/160°C fan-forced.

2 Boil, steam or microwave potato until tender; drain. Using fork, crush potato roughly.

3 Heat oil in large frying pan; cook garlic and onion, stirring, until onion softens. Add spices; cook, stirring, until fragrant. Add undrained tomatoes; cook, stirring, 5 minutes. Stir in potato and sultanas.

4 Make lengthways slit in each chilli, stopping 1cm from top and bottom, taking care not to cut all the way through; remove and discard seeds and membranes. Divide potato filling among chilli cavities. Place chillies on oiled oven tray; roast, covered, 30 minutes. Uncover; roast 20 minutes.

5 Make raita by combining cucumber and yogurt in small bowl. Serve chillies with raita and chapatis.

per serving 8.2g total fat (1.8g saturated fat); 1643kJ (393 cal), 59.5g carbohydrate; 13.8g protein; 11.9g fibre

steamed asian greens with char siu sauce

preparation time 5 minutes | cooking time 10 minutes | serves 4

1 fresh long red chilli, sliced thinly
350g broccolini, trimmed
150g snow peas, trimmed
2 baby buk choy (300g), halved
2 tablespoons char siu sauce
2 teaspoons sesame oil
1 tablespoon peanut oil
1 tablespoon toasted sesame seeds

1 Layer chilli, broccolini, snow peas and buk choy in baking-paper-lined bamboo steamer. Steam, covered, over wok of simmering water about 5 minutes or until vegetables are just tender.

2 Combine vegetables, sauce and sesame oil in large bowl.

3 Heat peanut oil in small saucepan until hot; pour oil over vegetable mixture then toss to combine. Serve sprinkled with seeds.

per serving 9.5g total fat (1.4g saturated fat); 635kJ (152 cal); 7g carbohydrate; 6.6g protein; 6.6g fibre

tofu sang choy bow

preparation time 20 minutes (plus standing time) | cooking time 20 minutes | serves 4

900g firm silken tofu
peanut oil, for deep-frying
¼ cup (60ml) lemon juice
1 tablespoon grated palm sugar
1½ tablespoons dark soy sauce
1½ teaspoons sambal oelek
1 medium red onion (170g), sliced thinly
2 lebanese cucumbers (260g), seeded, sliced thinly
1 cup (80g) bean sprouts
¼ cup firmly packed thai basil leaves
½ cup firmly packed fresh coriander leaves
8 large iceberg lettuce leaves

1 Pat tofu dry with absorbent paper; cut into 1.5cm cubes. Spread tofu, in single layer, on absorbent-paper-lined tray; cover tofu with more absorbent paper. Stand tofu 1 hour, changing paper after 30 minutes.

2 Heat oil in wok; deep-fry tofu, in batches, until browned lightly. Drain on absorbent paper.

3 Combine juice, sugar, sauce and sambal in small jug; stir until sugar dissolves.

4 Combine tofu in large bowl with onion, cucumber, sprouts, herbs and dressing.

5 Serve tofu mixture divided among lettuce leaves.

per serving 28g total fat (4.5g saturated fat); 1814kJ (434 cal); 12.1g carbohydrate; 30.5g protein; 7.5g fibre

dhal and paneer vegetable curry

preparation time 25 minutes | cooking time 1 hour 15 minutes | serves 4

You will need about a quarter of a small cabbage for this recipe.

2 tablespoons ghee
1 medium brown onion (150g), chopped finely
2 cloves garlic, crushed
2cm piece fresh ginger (10g), grated
2 teaspoons ground cumin
1 tablespoon ground coriander
1 teaspoon ground turmeric
2 teaspoons garam masala
2 cardamom pods, bruised
2 tablespoons mild curry paste
1 cup (200g) yellow split peas
810g can crushed tomatoes
2 cups (500ml) vegetable stock
2 cups (500ml) water
250g cabbage, chopped coarsely
2 medium carrots (240g), cut into 2cm pieces
½ cup (60g) frozen peas
2 x 100g packets paneer cheese, cut into 2cm pieces
⅓ cup loosely packed fresh coriander leaves

1   Heat ghee in large saucepan; cook onion, garlic and ginger, stirring, until onion softens. Add spices; cook, stirring, until fragrant. Add curry paste; cook, stirring, until fragrant.

2   Add split peas, undrained tomatoes, stock and the water; bring to a boil. Reduce heat; simmer, covered, 30 minutes, stirring occasionally. Uncover, add cabbage and carrot; cook, stirring occasionally, about 30 minutes or until split peas soften.

3   Add frozen peas and cheese; cook, uncovered, about 5 minutes or until cheese is heated through. Serve curry sprinkled with coriander.

per serving 20.1g total fat (10g saturated fat); 1923kJ (460 cal); 39.6g carbohydrate; 23.4g protein; 14.2g fibre

PANEER *is an Indian homemade farm cheese made from cow's milk. White in colour and soft in texture, this mild-flavoured cheese is similar to a dry version of ricotta or cottage cheese.*

age-dashi tofu

preparation time 15 minutes (plus standing time) | cooking time 30 minutes | serves 4

*Age-dashi (pronounced ah-gah dah-she], a simple dish of
deep-fried tofu in a flavourful dressing, is a popular entrée
in both Japanese restaurants and homes.
Bonito flakes can be found in most Asian food stores.*

300g firm tofu
1 teaspoon instant dashi
1 cup (250ml) hot water
1 tablespoon sake
1 tablespoon mirin
1½ tablespoons light soy sauce
2 tablespoons cornflour
1 tablespoon toasted sesame seeds
vegetable oil, for deep-frying
2 tablespoons coarsely grated daikon
1cm piece fresh ginger (5g), grated
2 green onions, chopped finely
2 teaspoons dried bonito flakes

1   Press tofu between two chopping boards with weight on top,
raise one end; stand 25 minutes.

2   Meanwhile, combine dashi and the water in small saucepan.
Add sake, mirin and sauce; bring to a boil. Remove from heat.

3   Cut tofu into eight even-sized pieces; pat dry between layers
of absorbent paper then toss in combined cornflour and sesame
seeds. Heat oil in wok; deep-fry tofu, in batches, until browned
lightly. Drain on absorbent paper.

4   Place two pieces of tofu in each serving bowl. Divide daikon,
ginger and onion among bowls; pour dashi dressing over tofu
then sprinkle with bonito flakes.

per serving 10.5g total fat (1.4g saturated fat); 715kJ (171 cal);
6.4g carbohydrate; 10.2g protein; 1.8g fibre

DASHI *is the basic fish and seaweed stock that
accounts for the distinctive flavour of many
Japanese dishes. It is made from dried bonito
(mackerel) flakes and kombu (kelp). Instant
dashi powder, also known as dashi-no-moto,
can be purchased in concentrated liquid or
granule form; here, we used granulated dashi.*

tomato rice

preparation time 15 minutes | cooking time 30 minutes | serves 4

2 tablespoons peanut oil

1 medium brown onion (150g), chopped finely

2 cloves garlic, crushed

3 medium tomatoes (450g), peeled, seeded, chopped finely

2 tablespoons tomato paste

4 cloves

2 cups (400g) white long-grain rice

3 cups (750ml) water

1 Heat oil in medium saucepan; cook onion, garlic, tomato, paste and cloves, uncovered, about 10 minutes or until mixture is thick and pulpy.

2 Stir in rice and the water; bring to a boil. Reduce heat; cook, covered tightly, over low heat, about 15 minutes or until water is absorbed. Remove from heat; stand, covered, 10 minutes. Fluff rice with fork. Serve sprinkled with coriander, and warmed chapati, if you like.

per serving 9.8g total fat (1.8g saturated); 1973kJ (472 cal); 84.5g carbohydrate; 8.7g protein; 3.3g fibre

kaffir lime and rice salad with tofu and cashews

preparation time 20 minutes | cooking time 10 minutes | serves 4

We used a cryovac-packed ready-to-serve sweet chilli tofu in this recipe; there are various flavours of already marinated tofu pieces that can be found in the refrigerated section of most supermarkets and Asian food stores.

2 cups (400g) jasmine rice

2 fresh kaffir lime leaves, chopped finely

2 fresh long red chillies, chopped finely

2cm piece fresh ginger (10g), grated

400g packaged marinated tofu pieces, sliced thickly

½ cup coarsely chopped fresh coriander

1 large carrot (180g), cut into matchsticks

3 green onions, sliced thinly

¾ cup (120g) roasted unsalted cashews, chopped coarsely

lime and palm sugar dressing

1 teaspoon finely grated lime rind

½ cup (125ml) lime juice

2 tablespoons grated palm sugar

2 tablespoons fish sauce

1 Cook rice in large saucepan of boiling water, uncovered, until tender; drain. Rinse under cold water; drain.

2 Meanwhile, make lime and palm sugar dressing.

3 Combine rice, lime leaves, chilli, ginger, tofu, coriander, carrot, half the onion, ½ cup nuts and dressing in large bowl. Serve salad sprinkled with remaining onion and nuts.

lime and palm sugar dressing Combine ingredients in screw-top jar; shake well.

per serving 22.2g total fat (3.7g saturated fat); 2847kJ (681 cal); 90.9g carbohydrate; 25.6g protein; 6.3g fibre

lamb biryani

preparation time 20 minutes (plus refrigeration time) | cooking time 2 hours 15 minutes | serves 4

1kg lamb shoulder, cut into 3cm pieces
3cm piece fresh ginger (15g), grated
2 cloves garlic, crushed
2 fresh small red thai chillies, chopped finely
2 teaspoons garam masala
1 tablespoon finely chopped fresh coriander
¼ teaspoon ground turmeric
½ cup (140g) yogurt
2 tablespoons ghee
½ cup (40g) flaked almonds
¼ cup (40g) sultanas
2 medium brown onions (300g), sliced thickly
½ cup (125ml) water
pinch saffron threads
1 tablespoon hot milk
1½ cups (300g) basmati rice
¼ cup firmly packed fresh coriander leaves

1   Combine lamb, ginger, garlic, chilli, garam masala, chopped coriander, turmeric and yogurt in medium bowl, cover; refrigerate overnight.

2   Heat half the ghee in large saucepan; cook nuts and sultanas, stirring, until nuts brown lightly. Remove from pan.

3   Heat remaining ghee in same pan; cook onion, covered, 5 minutes. Uncover; cook, stirring occasionally, about 5 minutes or until browned lightly. Reserve half of the onion.

4   Add lamb mixture to pan; cook, stirring, until browned. Add the water; bring to a boil. Reduce heat; simmer, covered, 1 hour. Uncover; simmer about 30 minutes or until lamb is tender and sauce is thickened.

5   Meanwhile, combine saffron and milk in small bowl; stand 15 minutes.

6   Cook rice in medium saucepan of boiling water, uncovered, 5 minutes; drain.

7   Preheat oven to 180°C/160°C fan-forced.

8   Spread half the lamb mixture into oiled deep 2-litre (8-cup) ovenproof dish. Layer with half the rice; top with remaining lamb mixture then remaining rice. Drizzle milk mixture over rice; cover tightly with greased foil and lid. Bake about 30 minutes or until rice is tender.

9   Serve biryani topped with reserved onion, nut and sultana mixture and coriander leaves.

per serving 38.6g total fat (17.4g saturated fat); 3703kJ (886 cal); 73.8g carbohydrate; 58.7g protein; 3.4g fibre

tip | It could be said that there are as many types of biryani as there are grains of rice in this dish; Indians, Pakistanis as well as Bangladeshis all have their own version of biryani. Serve with raita, if you like.

crab and soba salad
with ginger miso dressing

preparation time 10 minutes | cooking time 20 minutes | serves 4

270g soba noodles

1 lebanese cucumber (130g), seeded, sliced thinly

1 small red onion (100g), chopped finely

1 medium carrot (120g), cut into matchsticks

50g baby spinach leaves, sliced thinly

400g fresh crab meat

1 tablespoon drained pickled ginger, sliced thinly

ginger miso dressing

6cm piece fresh ginger (30g), chopped coarsely

2 tablespoons drained pickled ginger

2 cloves garlic

⅓ cup (100g) yellow miso paste

½ teaspoon wasabi paste

½ cup (125ml) rice vinegar

½ cup (125ml) vegetable oil

2 tablespoons water

1 Make ginger miso dressing.

2 Cook noodles in large saucepan of boiling water, uncovered, until just tender; drain. Rinse under cold water; drain.

3 Combine noodles in large bowl with cucumber, onion, carrot, spinach, half the crab and half the dressing.

4 Divide salad among serving plates; top with remaining crab, ginger and remaining dressing.

ginger miso dressing Blend or process ingredients until smooth.

per serving 32.4g total fat (4g saturated fat); 2805kJ (671 cal); 55.9g carbohydrate; 35.9g protein; 5.9g fibre

beef kway teow

preparation time 10 minutes | cooking time 10 minutes | serves 4.

¼ cup (60ml) oyster sauce

2 tablespoons kecap manis

2 tablespoons chinese cooking wine

1 teaspoon sambal oelek

3 cloves garlic, crushed

2cm piece fresh ginger (10g), grated

2 tablespoons peanut oil

500g beef strips

450g fresh wide rice noodles

6 green onions, cut into 2cm lengths

1 small red capsicum (150g), sliced thinly

1 small green capsicum (150g), sliced thinly

¼ cup coarsely chopped garlic chives

2 cups (160g) bean sprouts

1 Combine sauces, wine, sambal, garlic and ginger in small jug.

2 Heat half the oil in wok; stir-fry beef, in batches, until browned lightly.

3 Place noodles in large heatproof bowl, cover with boiling water; separate with fork, drain.

4 Heat remaining oil in wok; stir-fry onion and capsicums until tender.

5 Return beef to wok with sauce mixture, noodles, chives and sprouts; stir-fry until hot.

per serving 17.7g total fat (4.8g saturated fat); 2195kJ (525 cal); 53g carbohydrate; 34.4g protein; 3.8g fibre

gulab jaman

preparation time 20 minutes (plus standing time) | cooking time 15 minutes | makes 24

A popular sweet eaten throughout India and Pakistan, traditionally during Eid, the post-Ramadan holiday, gulab jaman is always made with powdered milk, which gives it a cake-like texture.

2 cups (500ml) water
2 cups (440g) caster sugar
8 cardamom pods, bruised
2 cinnamon sticks
3 star anise
1 teaspoon rosewater
½ cup (75g) self-raising flour
¼ cup (25g) full-cream milk powder
125g spreadable cream cheese
24 raisins
vegetable oil, for deep-frying

1   Stir the water, sugar and spices in medium saucepan over heat, without boiling, until sugar dissolves. Bring to a boil; boil, uncovered, without stirring, 5 minutes. Remove from heat; stir in rosewater. Cool.

2   Combine flour, milk powder and cream cheese in medium bowl; mix to a soft dough. Turn onto floured surface; knead about 10 minutes. Roll 1 heaped teaspoon of dough around each raisin.

3   Heat oil in wok; deep-fry balls, in batches, until golden brown. Drain on absorbent paper. Place gulab jaman in syrup; stand 1 hour before serving.

per gulab jaman 2.5g total fat (1.4g saturated fat); 477kJ (144 cal); 21.4g carbohydrate; 1g protein; 0.1g fibre

almond and rosewater jelly

preparation time 20 minutes (plus standing and refrigeration time) | cooking time 15 minutes | serves 4

3 cups (750ml) milk
1½ cups (240g) blanched almonds
⅓ cup (75g) caster sugar
3½ teaspoons gelatine
1 teaspoon rosewater
2 passionfruits
1 medium mango (430g), chopped coarsely
1 starfruit (160g), sliced thinly
565g can lychees, rinsed, drained

1   Grease 8cm x 26cm bar cake pan.

2   Blend milk, nuts and sugar until mixture forms a smooth puree. Transfer to medium saucepan; heat until hot but not boiling. Remove from heat; stand 1 hour.

3   Pour mixture into large jug; strain through muslin-lined sieve into same cleaned pan; discard solids. Sprinkle gelatine over mixture; stir over heat, without boiling, until dissolved. Remove from heat, stir in rosewater; pour mixture into pan. Cover; refrigerate 3 hours or overnight.

4   Scoop pulp from passionfruit into medium bowl with remaining fruit; toss to combine.

5   Turn jelly onto chopping board, cut into 24 cubes. Serve jelly with fruit.

per serving 41.2g total fat (6.9g saturated fat); 2955kJ (707 cal); 56.1g carbohydrate; 23g protein; 11.2g fibre

passionfruit and coconut crème brûlèe

preparation time 15 minutes (plus refrigeration time) | cooking time 50 minutes | serves 4

Use ice in the baking dish to help keep the custard cold while grilling the sugar topping. You need three passionfruits for this recipe.

1 egg
2 egg yolks
2 tablespoons caster sugar
¼ cup (60ml) passionfruit pulp
280ml can coconut cream
½ cup (125ml) cream
1 tablespoon brown sugar

1 Preheat oven to 180°C/160°C fan-forced.

2 Combine egg, egg yolks, caster sugar and passionfruit in medium heatproof bowl.

3 Combine coconut cream and cream in small saucepan; bring to a boil. Gradually whisk hot cream mixture into egg mixture. Place bowl over medium saucepan of simmering water; stir over heat about 10 minutes or until custard thickens slightly.

4 Divide custard among four deep ½-cup (125ml) heatproof dishes. Place dishes in large baking dish; pour enough boiling water into baking dish to come halfway up sides of dishes. Bake, uncovered, about 30 minutes or until custards set. Remove custards from water; cool. Cover; refrigerate 3 hours or overnight.

5 Preheat grill. Place custards in shallow flameproof dish filled with ice cubes. Sprinkle each custard with 1 teaspoon brown sugar; using finger, gently smooth sugar over the surface of each custard. Place baking dish under grill until tops of crème brûlèe caramelise.

per serving 30.3g total fat (21.6g saturated fat); 1526kJ (365 cal); 16.7g carbohydrate; 5.7g protein; 3.3g fibre

pistachio, honey and cardamom kulfi

preparation time 10 minutes (plus cooling and freezing time) | cooking time 15 minutes | serves 4

2 x 375ml cans evaporated milk
¾ cup (180ml) cream
3 cardamom pods, bruised
2 tablespoons honey
⅓ cup (45g) finely chopped roasted pistachios
2 tablespoons coarsely chopped roasted pistachios

1 Combine milk, cream and cardamom in large heavy-based saucepan; bring to a boil. Reduce heat; simmer, uncovered, stirring occasionally, about 10 minutes or until reduced to about 3 cups. Stir in honey, remove from heat; cool 15 minutes.

2 Strain mixture into large bowl; discard cardamom. Divide kulfi mixture among four ¾-cup (180ml) moulds; sprinkle with finely chopped nuts. Cover with foil; freeze 3 hours or overnight.

3 Turn kulfi onto serving plates; sprinkle with coarsely chopped nuts to serve.

per serving 45.1g total fat (25.6g saturated fat); 2621kJ (627 cal); 36.3g carbohydrate; 19.3g protein; 1.7g fibre

tip | Lumpia, eaten throughout Indonesia and the Philippines as snacks, are somewhat similar to spring rolls or burritos, and can be sweet or savoury.

banana lumpia with brown sugar syrup and coconut ice-cream

preparation time 20 minutes (plus freezing time) | cooking time 15 minutes | makes 12

1 cup (250ml) water
¼ cup (55g) brown sugar
¼ cup (55g) caster sugar
1 vanilla bean, split lengthways
2 star anise
2 tablespoons white sugar
2 teaspoons ground cinnamon
1 tablespoon cornflour
1 tablespoon water, extra
3 small ripe bananas (390g)
12 small (12.5cm x 12.5cm) spring roll wrappers
vegetable oil, for deep-frying
¾ cup (35g) toasted flaked coconut

coconut ice-cream
1 cup (75g) toasted shredded coconut
¼ cup (60ml) coconut-flavoured liqueur
1 litre vanilla ice-cream, softened

1 Make coconut ice-cream.

2 Stir the water, brown sugar, caster sugar, vanilla bean and star anise in small saucepan over heat, without boiling, until sugar dissolves. Bring to a boil; boil, uncovered, without stirring, about 15 minutes or until syrup thickens. Remove and discard solids.

3 Meanwhile, combine white sugar and cinnamon in small bowl. Blend cornflour with the extra water in another small bowl.

4 Quarter each banana lengthways. Centre 1 piece of banana on each wrapper then sprinkle each with about ½ teaspoon cinnamon sugar. Fold wrapper over banana ends then roll wrapper to enclose filling. Brush edges with cornflour mixture to seal.

5 Heat oil in wok; deep-fry lumpia, in batches, until golden brown and crisp. Drain on absorbent paper. Sprinkle with combined remaining cinnamon sugar and coconut, drizzle with syrup; serve with ice cream.

coconut ice-cream Fold coconut and liqueur through slightly softened ice-cream, cover; freeze about 3 hours or overnight.

per lumpia and ⅓ cup ice-cream 9.9g total fat (6.9g saturated fat); 882kJ (211 cal); 24.8g carbohydrate; 2.4g protein; 1.5g fibre

green tea ice-cream with fruit salsa

preparation time 15 minutes (plus refrigeration and freezing time) | cooking time 10 minutes | serves 4

2 tablespoons green tea powder

2 tablespoons boiling water

1 tablespoon caster sugar

1 vanilla bean

1 cup (250ml) milk

2 egg yolks

¼ cup (55g) caster sugar, extra

300ml thickened cream, whipped

10 fresh lychees (250g), chopped finely

2 medium kiwifruits (170g), chopped finely

½ small papaya (325g), chopped finely

1 tablespoon finely chopped fresh mint

1   Combine tea, the water and sugar in small bowl; stand 10 minutes.

2   Split vanilla bean lengthways; scrape out seeds. Combine pod, seeds and milk in small saucepan; bring to a boil. Stir in tea mixture; stand 5 minutes.

3   Meanwhile, whisk egg yolks and extra sugar in small bowl until creamy; gradually whisk into hot milk mixture. Stir over low heat, without boiling, until mixture thickens slightly.

4   Strain mixture into medium heatproof bowl; discard pod. Cover surface of custard with plastic wrap; cool. Refrigerate about 1 hour or until cold.

5   Fold whipped cream into cold custard. Pour mixture into ice-cream maker; churn according to manufacturer's instructions (or place custard in shallow container, cover with foil; freeze until almost firm). Place ice-cream in large bowl, chop coarsely then beat with electric mixer until smooth. Cover; freeze until firm. Repeat process twice more.

6   Combine fruit and mint in small bowl. Serve ice-cream with salsa.

per serving 33.5g total fat (20.9g saturated fat); 2123kJ (508 cal); 43.7g carbohydrate; 6.9g protein; 3.3g fibre

VANILLA BEAN *a long, dried thin pod from a tropical golden orchid grown in Central and South America and Tahiti; the minuscule black seeds inside the bean are used to impart a luscious vanilla flavour in baking and desserts. A whole bean can be placed in the sugar container to make vanilla sugar.*

Clockwise from top left:
kaffir lime sorbet, lemon grass
sorbet, blood orange sorbet

lemon grass sorbet

preparation time 20 minutes (plus cooling and freezing time) | cooking time 10 minutes | serves 8

2 x 10cm sticks fresh lemon grass (40g),
    chopped finely
1 cup (220g) caster sugar
2½ cups (625ml) water
¾ cup (180ml) lemon juice
yellow food colouring
1 egg white

1   Stir lemon grass, sugar and the water in medium saucepan over high heat until sugar dissolves; bring to a boil. Reduce heat; simmer, uncovered, without stirring, 5 minutes. Transfer to large heatproof jug, cool to room temperature; stir in juice and tint pale yellow with food colouring.

2   Pour sorbet mixture into 14cm x 21cm loaf pan, cover tightly with foil; freeze 3 hours or overnight. Process mixture with egg white until smooth. Return to pan, cover; freeze until firm.
per serving 0g total fat (0g saturated fat); 489kJ (117 cal); 28.1g carbohydrate; 0.6g protein; 0g fibre

blood orange sorbet

preparation time 20 minutes (plus cooling and freezing time) | cooking time 10 minutes | serves 8

3 teaspoons finely grated blood orange rind
1 cup (220g) caster sugar
2½ cups (625ml) water
¾ cup (180ml) blood orange juice
red food colouring
1 egg white

1   Stir rind, sugar and the water in medium saucepan over high heat until sugar dissolves; bring to a boil. Reduce heat; simmer, uncovered, without stirring, 5 minutes. Transfer to large heatproof jug, cool to room temperature; stir in juice and tint with food colouring.

2   Pour sorbet mixture into 14cm x 21cm loaf pan, cover tightly with foil; freeze 3 hours or overnight. Process mixture with egg white until smooth. Return to pan, cover; freeze until firm.
per serving 0g total fat (0g saturated fat); 510kJ (122 cal), 29.4g carbohydrate; 0.6g protein; 0.1g fibre

kaffir lime sorbet

preparation time 20 minutes (plus cooling and freezing time) | cooking time 10 minutes | serves 8

3 fresh kaffir lime leaves, chopped finely
1 cup (220g) caster sugar
2½ cups (625ml) water
¾ cup (180ml) lime juice
green food colouring
1 egg white

1   Stir lime leaves, sugar and the water in medium saucepan over high heat until sugar dissolves; bring to a boil. Reduce heat; simmer, uncovered, without stirring, 5 minutes. Transfer to large heatproof jug, cool to room temperature; stir in juice and tint pale green with food colouring.

2   Pour sorbet mixture into 14cm x 21cm loaf pan, cover tightly with foil; freeze 3 hours or overnight. Process mixture with egg white until smooth. Return to pan, cover; freeze until firm.
per serving 0g total fat (0g saturated fat); 485kJ (116 cal); 27.8g carbohydrate; 0.6g protein; 0g fibre

glossary

BEAN CURD POUCHES see page 14.

BREADCRUMBS

japanese also known as panko; available in two kinds: larger pieces and fine crumbs; have a lighter texture than Western-style breadcrumbs. Available from Asian food stores and some supermarkets, and unless you make rather coarse breadcrumbs from stale white bread that's either quite stale or gently toasted, nothing is an adequate substitution.

stale crumbs made by grating, blending or processing 1- or 2-day-old bread.

BROCCOLINI a cross between broccoli and gai lan, is milder and sweeter than traditional broccoli. Substitute with gai lan or common broccoli.

CAPSICUM also known as bell pepper or, simply, pepper. Discard seeds and membranes before use.

CARDAMOM has a distinctive aromatic, sweetly rich flavour and is one of the world's most expensive spices. Can be purchased in pod, seed or ground form.

CHILLI available in many different types, fresh or dried. Use rubber gloves when seeding and chopping fresh chillies, as they can burn your skin. Removing seeds and membranes lessens the heat level.

CHINESE COOKING WINE see page 53.

GARLIC CHIVES have rougher, flatter leaves than plain chives, and a pink-tinged teardrop-shaped flowering bud at the end.

CORIANDER see page 37.

CUMIN also known as zeera.

DASHI see page 86.

EGG if a recipe calls for raw or barely cooked eggs, exercise caution if there is a salmonella problem in your area.

EGGPLANT also known as aubergine; also available char-grilled, packed in oil, in jars.

FIVE-SPICE a fragrant mixture of ground cinnamon, cloves, star anise, sichuan peppercorns and fennel seeds. Also known as chinese five-spice.

FLOUR

besan also known as chickpea flour or gram; made from ground chickpeas.

cornflour also known as cornstarch.

plain also known as all-purpose flour.

self-raising also known as self-rising; an all-purpose plain flour with baking powder added in the proportion of 1 cup flour to 2 teaspoons baking powder.

GHEE or clarified butter; has the milk solids removed, so has a high smoking point (can be heated to a high temperature without burning).

GINGER when fresh, is also known as green or root ginger; the thick gnarled root of a tropical plant.

pickled ginger see page 41.

GREEN TEA POWDER green tea leaves ground into a fine powder; sold, ready-ground, in small tins in Asian food shops.

GYOZA WRAPPERS see page 11.

JAPANESE MUSTARD hot mustard available in ready-to-use paste in tubes or powder from Asian food shops.

KALONJI SEEDS also known as nigella; small angular purple-black seeds that are a creamy colour inside and possess a sharp, nutty taste. Found in spice shops and Middle-Eastern and Asian food stores.

LEBANESE CUCUMBER short, slender and thin-skinned. Has tender, edible skin, tiny, yielding seeds and a sweet taste.

MINCE MEAT also known as ground meat.

MIRIN a Japanese champagne-coloured cooking wine made of glutinous rice and alcohol expressly for cooking; not to be confused with sake.

NOODLES

bean thread (wun sen) made from mung bean paste; also known as cellophane or glass noodles because they are transparent when cooked. White in colour (not off-white like rice vermicelli), very delicate and fine; available dried in various sized bundles.

egg (ba mee) also known as yellow noodles; made from wheat flour and eggs; sold fresh and dried. Range in size from thin strands to wide, thick spaghetti-like pieces.

fresh rice see page 99.

hokkien also known as stir-fry noodles; fresh wheat flour noodles resembling thick, yellow-brown spaghetti.

rice stick see page 95.

soba thin Japanese noodles made from buckwheat and wheat flour.

thin wheat see page 100.

PALM SUGAR also known as nam tan pip, jaggery, jawa or gula melaka; made from the sap of the sugar palm tree. Light brown to black in colour and usually sold in rock-hard cakes; often grated before use. Substitute brown sugar, if preferred.

PAPAYA, GREEN see page 73.

PASTE

curry many prepared curry pastes are available in mild, medium or hot varieties in supermarkets. Green curry paste is one of the most popular Thai pastes, along with red, massaman, panang and yellow, while korma, tikka and madras are a few of the better known Indian ones.

shrimp see page 26.

yellow bean a salty brown thin paste made from fermented soybeans (yellow beans).

yellow miso a thick paste made from fermented and processed soybeans and rice; a deep yellow, smooth miso with a fairly salty but tart flavour.

PANEER CHEESE *see page 85.*
PICKLED GINGER *see page 41.*
RICE
basmati fragrant long-grained white rice.
black also known as purple rice because, although a deep charcoal black in colour when raw, it turns a purplish-black colour after cooking. A medium-grain unmilled rice, with a nutty, whole-grain flavour and crunchy bite.
jasmine a long-grained white rice with a perfumed aromatic quality; white rice can be substituted but the taste will not be the same.
koshihikari small, round-grain white rice. If unavailable, substitute a white short-grain rice such as arborio and cook using the absorption method.
ROSEWATER EXTRACT made from crushed rose petals; available from health food stores and Middle Eastern food stores.
SAGO a grain often used in puddings and desserts; similar to tapioca but sourced from a variety of palm, while tapioca is from the root of the cassava plant.
SAKE Japan's favourite rice wine is used in cooking, marinating and as part of dipping sauces. If sake is unavailable, dry sherry, vermouth or brandy can be used as a substitute. *Cooking sake* is made exclusively for use in cooking and should not be consumed as a beverage.
SAMBAL OELEK (also spelled ulek or olek) Indonesian in origin; made from ground chillies and vinegar.
SAUCES
char siu also known as chinese barbecue sauce. A dark-red-brown paste-like ingredient with a sweet, spicy flavour. Made with fermented soybeans, honey and various spices.

fish also called naam pla or nuoc naam. Made from pulverised salted fermented fish (most often anchovies); has a strong taste and pungent smell, so use according to your taste.
hoisin a rich, dark, sweet barbecue sauce made from soybeans, chillies, red beans and spices.
japanese worcestershire there are two types available, one similar to normal worcestershire and the other somewhat blander; both are made from varying proportions of vinegar, tomatoes, onions, carrots, garlic and spices.
kecap asin, kecap manis *see soy sauce.*
oyster thick, richly flavoured brown sauce made from oysters and their brine; cooked with salt and soy sauce, and thickened with starches.
soy *see soy sauce.*
sweet chilli a mild sauce made from red chillies, sugar, garlic and vinegar.
SHALLOT also called french shallot, golden shallot or eschalot; elongated, small, brown-skinned members of the onion family.
fried found in cellophane bags or jars at Asian grocery shops; sprinkled over just-cooked food. Once opened, will keep for months if stored tightly seeled. Make your own by frying thinly sliced peeled shallots or baby onions until golden brown and crisp.
purple are thin-layered and intensely flavoured. Also known as asian shallots; related to the onion, but resembles garlic (they grow in bulbs of multiple cloves).
SICHUAN PEPPERCORNS also known as szechuan or chinese peppercorns; have a distinctive peppery-lemon flavour.
SNAKE BEANS *see page 66.*

SOY SAUCE made from fermented soybeans. Several variations are available in supermarkets and Asian food stores.
dark deep brown, almost black in colour; rich, with a thicker consistency than other types. Pungent but not particularly salty, it is good for marinating.
japanese an all-purpose low-sodium soy made with more wheat content than its Chinese counterparts. Possibly the best table soy and the one to choose if you only want one variety.
kecap asin a thick, dark, salty soy sauce.
kecap manis a thick, dark, sweet soy sauce.
light a light-coloured, salty-tasting, fairly thin sauce; Not to be confused with salt-reduced or low-sodium soy sauces.
STAR ANISE *see page 61.*
SUGAR BANANA smaller than the common variety; very sweet in flavour.
TAMARIND *see page 50.*
TOFU aso known as bean curd, an off-white, custard like product made from the milk of crushed soybeans; comes fresh as soft or firm, and processed as fried or pressed dried sheets. *Silken tofu* refers to the method by which it is made, where it is strained through silk.
VANILLA BEAN *see page 110.*
VINEGAR
red wine made from fermented red wine.
rice a colourless vinegar made from fermented rice and flavoured with sugar and salt. Also known as seasoned rice vinegar. Sherry can be substituted.
white wine made from white wine.
WASABI an asian horseradish used to make the pungent, green-coloured sauce; sold in powdered or paste form.
ZUCCHINI also known as courgette (*see page 34*).

conversion chart

MEASURES

One Australian metric measuring cup holds approximately 250ml; one Australian metric tablespoon holds 20ml; one Australian metric teaspoon holds 5ml.

The difference between one country's measuring cups and another's is within a two- or three-teaspoon variance, and will not affect your cooking results. North America, New Zealand and the United Kingdom use a 15ml tablespoon.

All cup and spoon measurements are level. The most accurate way of measuring dry ingredients is to weigh them. When measuring liquids, use a clear glass or plastic jug with the metric markings.

We use large eggs with an average weight of 60g.

DRY MEASURES

METRIC	IMPERIAL
15g	½oz
30g	1oz
60g	2oz
90g	3oz
125g	4oz (¼lb)
155g	5oz
185g	6oz
220g	7oz
250g	8oz (½lb)
280g	9oz
315g	10oz
345g	11oz
375g	12oz (¾lb)
410g	13oz
440g	14oz
470g	15oz
500g	16oz (1lb)
750g	24oz (1½lb)
1kg	32oz (2lb)

LIQUID MEASURES

METRIC	IMPERIAL
30ml	1 fluid oz
60ml	2 fluid oz
100ml	3 fluid oz
125ml	4 fluid oz
150ml	5 fluid oz (¼ pint/1 gill)
190ml	6 fluid oz
250ml	8 fluid oz
300ml	10 fluid oz (½ pint)
500ml	16 fluid oz
600ml	20 fluid oz (1 pint)
1000ml (1 litre)	1¾ pints

LENGTH MEASURES

METRIC	IMPERIAL
3mm	⅛in
6mm	¼in
1cm	½in
2cm	¾in
2.5cm	1in
5cm	2in
6cm	2½in
8cm	3in
10cm	4in
13cm	5in
15cm	6in
18cm	7in
20cm	8in
23cm	9in
25cm	10in
28cm	11in
30cm	12in (1ft)

OVEN TEMPERATURES

These oven temperatures are only a guide for conventional ovens. For fan-forced ovens, check the manufacturer's manual.

	°C (CELSIUS)	°F (FAHRENHEIT)	GAS MARK
Very slow	120	250	½
Slow	150	275-300	1-2
Moderately slow	160	325	3
Moderate	180	350-375	4-5
Moderately hot	200	400	6
Hot	220	425-450	7-8
Very hot	240	475	9

ARE YOU MISSING SOME OF THE WORLD'S FAVOURITE COOKBOOKS?

The Australian Women's Weekly Cookbooks are available from bookshops, cookshops, supermarkets and other stores all over the world. You can also buy direct from the publisher, using the order form below.

TITLE	RRP	QTY	TITLE	RRP	QTY
100 Fast Fillets	£6.99		Japanese Cooking Class	£6.99	
Barbecue Meals In Minutes	£6.99		Just For One	£6.99	
Beginners Cooking Class	£6.99		Kids' Birthday Cakes	£6.99	
Beginners Simple Meals	£6.99		Kids Cooking	£6.99	
Beginners Thai	£6.99		Kids' Cooking Step-by-Step	£6.99	
Best Food Desserts	£6.99		Low-carb, Low-fat	£6.99	
Best Food Fast	£6.99		Low-fat Feasts	£6.99	
Best Food Mains	£6.99		Low-fat Food for Life	£6.99	
Cafe Classics	£6.99		Low-fat Meals in Minutes	£6.99	
Cakes, Bakes & Desserts	£6.99		Main Course Salads	£6.99	
Cakes Biscuits & Slices	£6.99		Mexican	£6.99	
Cakes Cooking Class	£6.99		Middle Eastern Cooking Class	£6.99	
Caribbean Cooking	£6.99		Midweek Meals in Minutes	£6.99	
Casseroles	£6.99		Moroccan & the Foods of North Africa	£6.99	
Casseroles & Slow-Cooked Classics	£6.99		Muffins, Scones & Breads	£6.99	
Cheap Eats	£6.99		New Casseroles	£6.99	
Cheesecakes: baked and chilled	£6.99		New Classics	£6.99	
Chicken	£6.99		New Curries	£6.99	
Chicken Meals in Minutes	£6.99		New Finger Food	£6.99	
Chinese & the Foods of Thailand,			New French Food	£6.99	
Vietnam, Malaysia & Japan	£6.99		New Food	£6.99	
Chinese Cooking Class	£6.99		New Salads	£6.99	
Christmas Cooking	£6.99		Party Food and Drink	£6.99	
Chocolate	£6.99		Pasta Meals in Minutes	£6.99	
Cocktails	£6.99		Potatoes	£6.99	
Cookies & Biscuits	£6.99		Salads: Simple, Fast & Fresh	£6.99	
Cooking for Friends	£6.99		Saucery	£6.99	
Cupcakes & Fairycakes	£6.99		Sauces Salsas & Dressings	£6.99	
Detox	£6.99		Sensational Stir-Fries	£6.99	
Dinner Lamb	£6.99		Slim	£6.99	
Dinner Seafood	£6.99		Soup	£6.99	
Easy Curry	£6.99		Stir-fry	£6.99	
Easy Spanish-Style	£6.99		Superfoods for Exam Success	£6.99	
Essential Soup	£6.99		Sweet Old-Fashioned Favourites	£6.99	
Food for Fit and Healthy Kids	£6.99		Tapas Mezze Antipasto & other bites	£6.99	
Foods of the Mediterranean	£6.99		Thai Cooking Class	£6.99	
Foods That Fight Back	£6.99		Traditional Italian	£6.99	
Fresh Food Fast	£6.99		Vegetarian Meals in Minutes	£6.99	
Fresh Food for Babies & Toddlers	£6.99		Vegie Food	£6.99	
Good Food for Babies & Toddlers	£6.99		Wicked Sweet Indulgences	£6.99	
Greek Cooking Class	£6.99		Wok, Meals in Minutes	£6.99	
Grills	£6.99				
Healthy Heart Cookbook	£6.99				
Indian Cooking Class	£6.99		TOTAL COST:	£	

Mr/Mrs/Ms _____

Address _____

_____ Postcode _____

Day time phone _____ email* (optional) _____

I enclose my cheque/money order for £ _____

or please charge £ _____

to my: ☐ Access ☐ Mastercard ☐ Visa ☐ Diners Club

Card number | | | | | | | | | | | | | | | | |

Expiry date _____ 3 digit security code *(found on reverse of card)* _____

Cardholder's name_____ Signature _____

* By including your email address, you consent to receipt of any email regarding this magazine, and other emails which inform you of ACP's other publications, products, services and events, and to promote third party goods and services you may be interested in.

To order: Mail or fax – photocopy or complete the order form above, and send your credit card details or cheque payable to: Australian Consolidated Press (UK), ACP Books, 10 Scirocco Close, Moulton Park Office Village, Northampton NN3 6AP.
phone (+44) (0)1604 642200
fax (+44) (0)1604 642300
email books@acpuk.com
or order online at www.acpuk.com
Non-UK residents: We accept the credit cards listed on the coupon, or cheques, drafts or International Money Orders payable in sterling and drawn on a UK bank. Credit card charges are at the exchange rate current at the time of payment.
Postage and packing UK: Add £1.00 per order plus £1.75 per book.
Postage and packing overseas: Add £2.00 per order plus £3.50 per book.
All pricing current at time of going to press and subject to change/availability.
Offer ends 31.12.2008

TEST KITCHEN
Food director Pamela Clark
Food editor Karen Hammial
Assistant food editor Sarah Schwikkard
Test Kitchen manager Cathie Lonnie
Senior home economist Elizabeth Macri
Home economists Belinda Farlow,
Miranda Farr, Nicole Jennings, Angela Muscat,
Rebecca Squadrito, Jacqui Storum, Kellie Thomas
Nutritional information Belinda Farlow

ACP BOOKS
Editorial director Susan Tomnay
Creative director Hieu Chi Nguyen
Designer Hannah Blackmore
Senior editor Wendy Bryant

Director of sales Brian Cearnes
Marketing manager Bridget Cody
Business analyst Ashley Davies
Production manager Cedric Taylor

Chief executive officer Ian Law
Group publisher Pat Ingram
General manager Christine Whiston
Editorial director (WW) Deborah Thomas

RIGHTS ENQUIRIES
Laura Bamford Director ACP Books
lbamford@acpuk.com

Produced by ACP Books, Sydney.
Printed by Dai Nippon, c/o Samhwa Printing Co. Ltd.
237-10 Kuro-dong, Kuro-ku, Seoul 152-053, Korea.
Published by ACP Books, a division of
ACP Magazines Ltd, 54 Park St, Sydney;
GPO Box 4088, Sydney, NSW 2001.
phone (02) 9282 8618 fax (02) 9267 9438.
acpbooks@acpmagazines.com.au
www.acpbooks.com.au

To order books, phone 136 116 (within Australia).
Send recipe enquiries to:
recipeenquiries@acpmagazines.com.au

Australia Distributed by Network Services,
phone +61 2 9282 8777 fax +61 2 9264 3278
networkweb@networkservicescompany.com.au
United Kingdom Distributed by Australian
Consolidated Press (UK),
phone (01604) 642 200 fax (01604) 642 300
books@acpuk.com
New Zealand Distributed by Netlink
Distribution Company,
phone (9) 366 9966 ask@ndc.co.nz
South Africa Distributed by PSD Promotions,
phone (27 11) 392 6065/7
fax (27 11) 392 6079/80
orders@psdprom.co.za

The Australian Women's Weekly
Chinese and the foods of Thailand, Vietnam,
Malaysia & Japan
Includes index.
ISBN 978 1 86396 652 8 (pbk).
1. Cookery, Asian.
I. Clark, Pamela. II Title: Australian Women's Weekly
641.595
© ACP Magazines Ltd 2007
ABN 18 053 273 546

The publishers would like to thank the following
for props used in photography: Riess Enamelware,
Crowley & Grouch Pty Ltd; Rhubarb, Richmond,
Victoria; That Vintage Shop, Marrickville, NSW;
Maxwell & Williams, Australia.

You'll find these books and more available on sale
at bookshops, cookshops, selected supermarkets or
direct from the publisher (order form on p119).